Stage 4 Paper 13

Strategic Financial Management

First edition 1996
Fourth edition January 1999

ISBN 0 7517 3482 9 (previous edition 0 7517 3451 9)

British Library Cataloguing-in-Publication Data

A catalogue record for this book
is available from the British Library

Published by

BPP Publishing Limited
Aldine House, Aldine Place
London W12 8AW

http://www.bpp.co.uk

Printed in Great Britain by Ashford Colour Press, Gosport, Hants.

If you use CIMA **Passcards**, you can be sure that the time you spend on final revision for your **1999 exams** is time well spent.

- They **save you time**: following the structure of the BPP Study Text for Paper 13, important facts on key exam topics are summarised for you
- They incorporate diagrams to kick start your memory
- They are pocket-sized: you can run through them **anytime** and **anywhere**

CIMA **Passcards** focus on the exam you will be facing.

- They highlight which topics have been examined - and when
- They provide you with suggestions on subject examinability, given past exams and the direction the examiner appears to be taking, in **exam focus points**
- They give you useful **exam hints** that can earn you those vital extra marks in the exam

Run through the complete set of **Passcards** as often as you can during your final revision period. The day before the exam, try to go through the **Passcards** again. You will then be well on your way to passing your exams. **Good luck!**

Contents

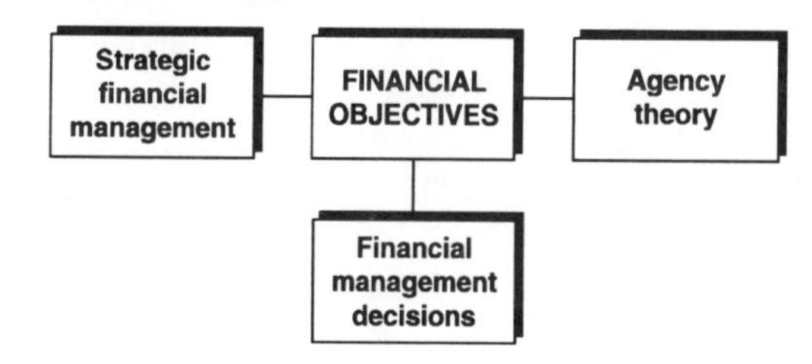

Strategic financial management

5/96, 11/96, 11/97, 11/98

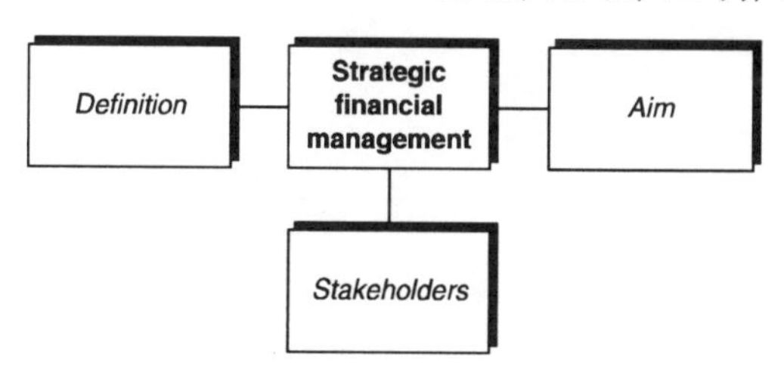

Definition

Strategy has been defined as 'a course of action, including the specification of the resources required, to achieve a specific objective'.

Strategic financial management is the area of strategy which falls within the scope of financial management, embracing *investment decisions, financing decisions* and *dividend decisions*.

Since strategy depends on the objectives or targets of the organisation or enterprise, a starting point for a study of strategic financial management is the identification and formulation of the objectives of the organisation or enterprise.

Aim

It is usually assumed that the aim of the financial manager in a business enterprise is to *maximise shareholders' wealth*. In studying financial management, we look at different ways of valuing a company and its shares.

In practice, factors affecting the market value of company shares include the following.

- Announcements of results
- Other information about the company's prospects, products, management
- Information about industry prospects
- Takeover speculation
- The state of the economy
- Exchange rate changes
- Interest rate changes
- New legislation

The following aspects of objectives may also need to be considered.

- Short-term v long-term objectives
- Private v public sector objectives
- Financial v non-financial objectives

Appropriate objectives in a public sector organisation may be the '3 Es':

- Economy
- Efficiency
- Effectiveness

- *By the Lands Tribunal*: s 84(1) of the LPA 1925 gives the Lands Tribunal powers to modify or discharge covenants in such circumstances as obsolescence.

Remedies for breach of covenant

- *Common law damages*: available when the original covenantee sues the original covenantor or when the assignee of the covenantee sues the original covenantor (*Surrey CC v Bredero Homes Ltd* (1993)).
- *Interlocutory injunction.*
- *Final injunction.*
- *Equitable damages – damages in lieu of an injunction under s 50 of the Supreme Court Act 1981*: for example, in *Wrotham Park Estate Ltd v Parkside Homes Ltd* (1974), damages in lieu of an injunction were awarded because to order demolition of a housing estate, which had been built in breach of covenant, would be a waste of good housing.

The following objectives are financial.

- Maximise sales
- Maximise profits
- Maximise directors' remuneration

The following objectives are non-financial.

- Provide for welfare of employees or management
- Contribute to society as a whole
- Provide a service to a specified standard
- Fulfil responsibilities to customers and suppliers

Stakeholders

Stakeholders other than shareholders have various different goals.

- *Trade creditors* will normally want timely payment, without jeopardising trading relationships
- *Long-term creditors* will want to minimise the risk of default on loans in deciding whether to grant them, and will want to receive payments due on loans granted
- *Employees* will have various objectives such as seeking the maximum reward obtainable for their work, and stability of employment
- *Government* has objectives relating to macroeconomic policymaking, and to political goals
- *Management* will want to maximise their own rewards, an objective which sometimes conflicts with management's delegated responsibilities to act in the interests of shareholders

Shareholder value analysis (SVA) may help to focus management on creation of shareholder value rather than short-term profitability.

In SVA, *value drivers* (eg sales growth/ margin/cost of capital) having greatest impact on the NPV of future cash flows are identified.

Agency theory

Directors and managers act as agents of the shareholders. The *agency problem* occurs when agents do not act in the best interests of their principals.

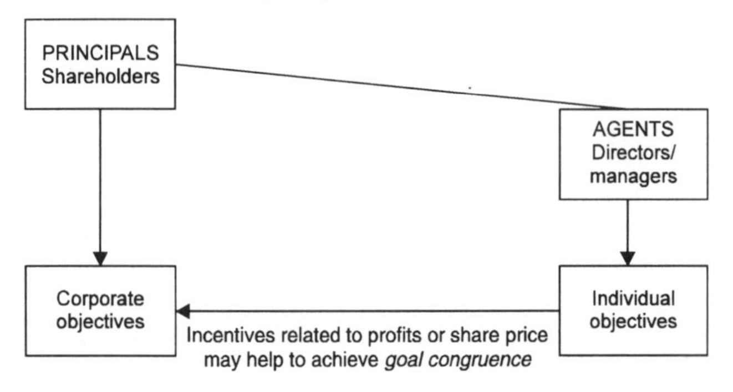

Incentives based on share price or profit (eg *profit-related pay* or *share options*) could encourage management to adopt *'creative accounting'* methods which will distort the reported performance of the company in the service of the managers' own ends.

But note that creative accounting methods like off-balance sheet finance present a temptation to management at all times as they allow a more favourable picture of the state of the company to be presented than otherwise.

Financial management decisions

11/95

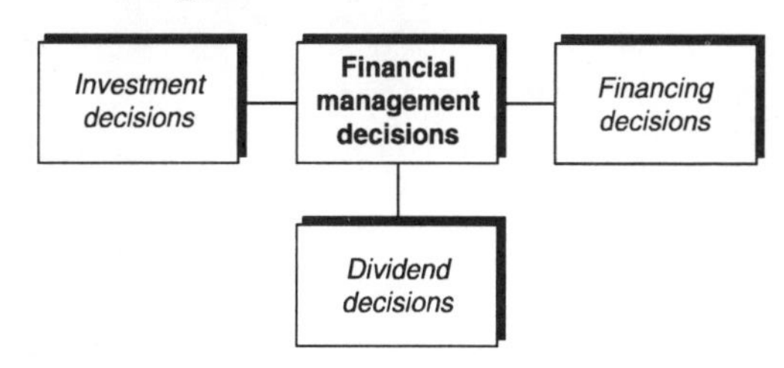

Investment decisions

Investment decisions are of various types. Examples are given below.

- Internal
  - Undertaking new projects
  - Investing in plant and machinery
  - Research and development
  - Advertising
- External
  - Takeovers
  - Mergers
  - Joint ventures
- Disinvestment
  - Shedding unprofitable business segments
  - Selling old plant and machinery
  - Selling subsidiaries

Financing decisions

Investments in assets must be funded. Financial management is concerned with how funds should be raised, in both the short and the long term, eg by:

- Retained earnings
- Issuing new shares
- Borrowing
- Taking more credit
- Leasing

An increasingly important aspect of the financial manager's expertise in making financing decisions is that of *risk management*.

Dividend decisions

Should the company pay out profits as dividends or retain them for investment to provide future growth?

In practice, the different types of decision distinguished above are interconnected and cannot be viewed in isolation.

> *Exam focus.* The topics covered in this chapter of these *Passcards* may well be examined along with other areas of the syllabus, as well as in discussion questions in their own right.

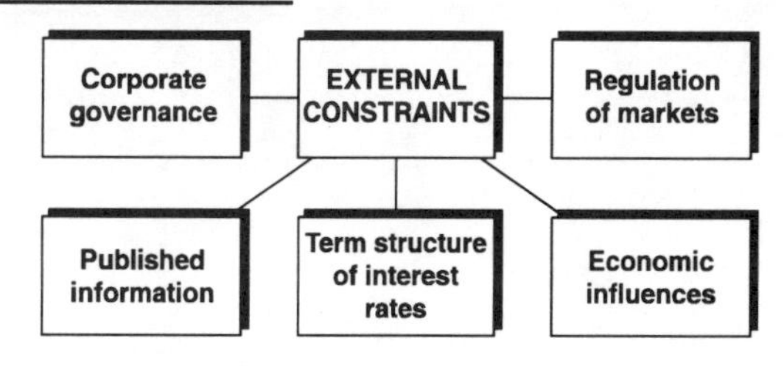

Exam focus. You are expected to bring to Paper 13 from your other studies a knowledge of UK accounting standards, although detailed accounting procedures will not be tested.

You should be broadly aware of the impact of legislation on business, although detailed knowledge of legislation is not required.

Corporate governance

Corporate governance is concerned with how companies are directed and controlled. Most companies are led by directors whose powers and responsibilities are set out in the Articles of Association.

International perspectives

The UK perspective on corporate governance can be contrasted with that of other countries.

- In the USA, stock exchange (SEC) regulation imposes stringent reporting requirements on listed US companies and requires all listed companies to have independent audit committees

- In Germany, a two-tier board system with separate management boards and supervisory boards is common
- Japanese companies enjoy a relatively low level of regulation
- In the UK, a voluntary Code of Best Practice has been established in the 1992 Cadbury Report

The Cadbury Code

Directors must state in the company's annual report whether they comply with the Cadbury Code, which covers the following points.

- The Board of Directors should meet regularly
- The separation of the posts of Chairman and Chief Executive is encouraged
- Non-executive directors should be independent, with no share options
- Executive directors' contracts should not run for more than three years (though the *Greenbury report* on directors' pay has recommended one year)
- Salaries are to be set by a remuneration committee, which Greenbury recommends should be made up solely of non-executive directors
- An audit committee reporting to the Board should appoint external auditors and regularly review audit work

Exam focus. For Paper 13, awareness of the Cadbury Report and its purposes and recommendations in outline is expected, but *not* detailed knowledge of its contents.

Regulation of markets

5/95, 5/97

The purpose of regulating markets is, in economists' terms, to prevent market failure - a situation in which a market fails to produce the optimal allocation of resources.

Examples of market failure - and possible policy responses:

- *Imperfect competition,* including *monopoly* - blocking of mergers against the public interest (eg by the UK Monopolies and Mergers Commission), controls over prices or the company's rate of return, 'windfall profits' taxes
- *Externalities* (costs imposed on third parties, such as pollution) - pollution controls, 'polluter pays' policies for environmental improvements
- *Imperfect consumer/worker information* - safety standards, job centres to ease labour market information flows
- *Failure of equity* or *social justice* - anti-discrimination or wage legislation, government-provided health care and education

Market controls including price controls may be overseen by an *industry regulator,* like those set up in the UK for privatised utilities (eg OFTEL, OFWAT).

Formulae which fix the regulated company's rate of return will limit incentive.

Economic influences

You will be aware of the various economic influences on business from earlier studies.

- The *fluctuations in aggregate demand* associated with the pattern of economic growth (the 'trade cycle') affect almost all businesses and their financial strategy

- *Inflation* affects production costs and selling prices in a market, and can in turn affect exchange rates, aggregate demand and interest rates

- *Exchange rate* changes continually alter the competitive position of importers and exports

- *Interest rates,* over which governments exert influence, affect the cost of borrowing, shareholders' expected returns and exchange rates

Treasury economic model

The UK Treasury's model of the economy:

- Consists of over 1,000 mathematical equations linking variables such as unemployment, the rate of inflation and the government's budget deficit

- Is designed to simulate how a set of policy actions such as interest rate changes affect variables such as consumer spending and job vacancies

Term structure of interest rates 5/96

Interest rates are, for corporate and individual borrowers, the cost of borrowing.

The *term structure of interest rates,* shown by the *yield curve,* refers to the way in which the yield on a security varies according to the term of the borrowing - that is, to the length of time until the debt matures.

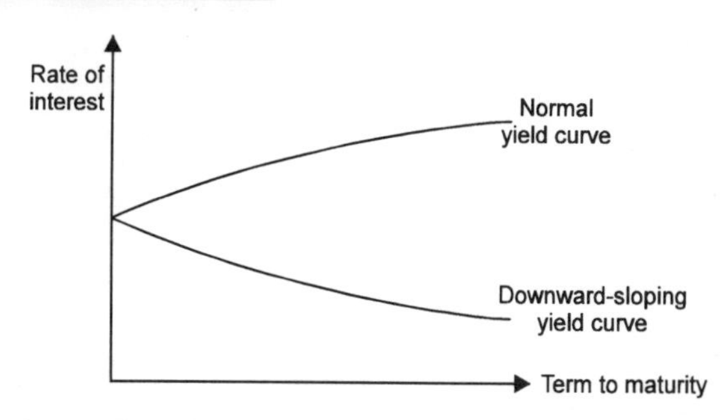

The 'normal' yield curve is upward sloping, reflecting the following factors.

- Investors' *liquidity preference* means that they demand a higher interest rate if their money is tied up for longer
- Investors' risk increases as the term of the lending becomes longer

The yield curve might have a different shape from the 'normal' curve at any time, for the following reasons.

Expectations of falling interest rates in the near future will reduce longer term rates as borrowers will be reluctant to borrow long-term at today's short-term rates. Expectations of rising rates will conversely result in a more upward slope on the yield curve.

Market segmentation theory suggests that the yield curve shape will be influenced by conditions in different market segments because groups of investors operate mainly within particular segments, eg banks and building societies in the short-term segment and life insurance companies and pension funds in long-term securities.

Market segmentation theory has some validity, but in practice interest rate expectations are treated as more significant.

Published information

5/96

Supplementing information which management obtains from internal sources and trade contacts are various forms of published information.

Examples:

- Newspapers and periodicals
- Trade journals
- Government statistics and publications
- Universities and colleges
- Databases

> *Exam focus.* As with Chapter 1, the topics covered in this chapter may well feature in questions in conjunction with topics from the rest of the syllabus.

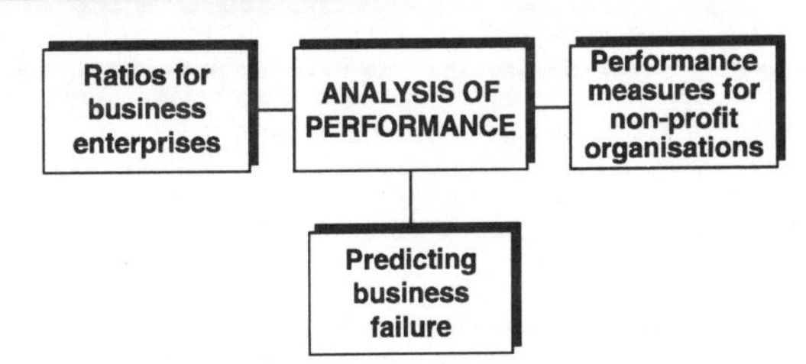

Analysis of performance

5/96, 5/97

Reasons for analysing a company's performance could be one of the following.

- To assess the company's financial position and potential for growth
- To spot weaknesses in the company's financial structure
- To assess the risk to an investor of holding either equity or debt capital in the company
- To assess the company's performance compared with other companies in the same industry or in general

Sources of information on individual enterprises include the following.

- Annual reports
- Financial data systems (Reuters, Extel etc)
- Companies House
- Stock Exchange Year Book
- Circulars
- Press and periodicals

Any ratio is fairly meaningless when considered alone. Useful comparisons can, however, be made with:

- The same company over different periods
- A company in a similar industry
- A company in a different industry

It may be necessary to make adjustments, for example for:

- The effect of inflation over time
- Different accounting policies
- Different ages of businesses, which may indicate different ages of fixed assets (distorting level of capital employed).

The *balanced scorecard* approach seeks to integrate traditional financial measures with operational, customer and staff perspectives.

> *Exam focus.* You may be expected to reconcile profit statements to cash flow statements, a skill you should have acquired in earlier studies.

Ratios for business enterprises

11/98

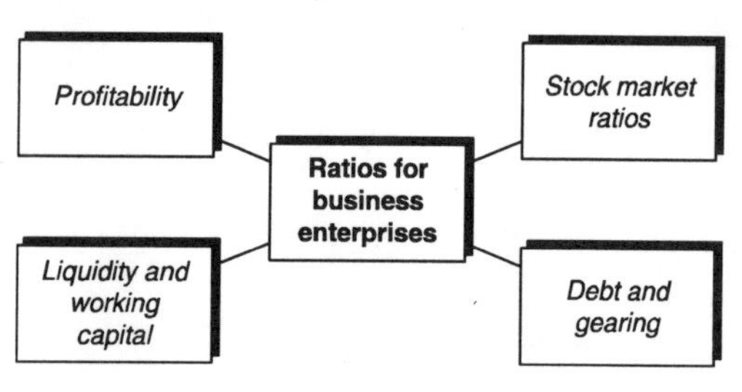

Profitability

The key *profitability* measure - return on capital employed (ROCE) - relates profit to the amount of funds used to make the profit.

$$\text{ROCE} = \frac{\text{Profit on ordinary activities before interest and taxation (PBIT)}}{\text{Capital employed}}$$

Capital employed = Shareholders' funds plus 'creditors: amounts falling due after more than one year' plus any long-term provisions for liabilities and charges

The following are also important measures for profit analysis.

- % growth in turnover
- Gross profit as % of turnover (gross profit margin)
- Net profit as % of turnover (net profit margin)

A *ratio pyramid* like that below shows the interrelationships between ratios and splits primary ratios down into secondary ratios.

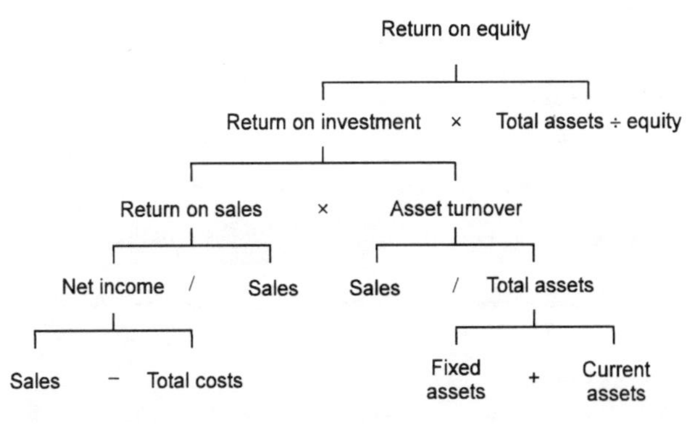

Stock market ratios

These are covered in Chapter 11 of these *Passcards*.

Liquidity and working capital

Short-term financial ratios include liquidity ratios (current ratio/acid test or quick ratio) and turnover periods. These are covered in Chapter 18.

Debt and gearing

Gearing is a measure of risk.

- Financial gearing is a measure of financial risk
- Operating gearing is a measure of business risk

A different measure of financial risk is the *debt ratio:* the ratio of a company's total debts to its total assets.

- Assets here consist of fixed assets at their balance sheet value, plus current assets
- Debts consist of all creditors, whether amounts falling due within one year or after more than one year

  (Ignore long-term provisions and liabilities, such as deferred taxation)

As a rule of thumb, if the debt ratio is above 50%, the debt position needs to be looked at more closely.

Operating gearing is concerned with the relationship in a company between its variable/fixed cost operating structure and its profitability. It can be calculated as the ratio of contribution (sales minus variable costs of sales) to PBIT.

The possibility of rises or falls in sales revenue and volumes means that operating gearing has possible implications for a company's business risk.

Financial gearing can be measured in a variety of ways, although every measure is a ratio of either:

- Prior charge capital to equity capital (including reserves), or
- Prior charge capital to total capital

Prior charge capital consists of preference shares as well as loan stock/debentures/mortgage loans.

- Short-term loans (less than one year to maturity) would generally be regarded as prior charge capital, although they are a current liability in the balance sheet, on the assumption that the loans will be replaced by new longer term loans when they mature
- Bank overdrafts (especially if there is a solid core overdraft) might be included in prior charge capital too

Equity capital or total capital might be valued by taking asset values as:

- Net book value/balance sheet value
- Net replacement cost
- Original gross cost
- Gross replacement cost
- Current cost/value

Financial gearing can also be measured for public limited companies by taking prior charge capital and equity capital at *market values*.

Another way of measuring a company's financial risk is to look at *interest cover*.

$$\text{Interest cover} = \frac{\text{PBIT}}{\text{Interest charges}}$$

A cover of less than three times indicates a very high level of financial risk.

> *Exam focus.* Skills in financial analysis using business ratios are often called for in exam questions. In allocating marks, the examiner will give at least as much weighting to the ability to choose and interpret appropriate indicators as to the ability to calculate the ratios correctly.

Performance measures for non-profit organisations 11/97

Non-profit organisations seek in their use of funds to achieve value for money, which can be expressed in terms of 3 Es.

- *Economy* - not spending £2 when the same thing can be bought for £1
- *Efficiency* - getting the best use out of what money is spent on
- *Effectiveness* - spending funds so as to achieve the organisation's objectives

Suitable performance measures for non-profit organisations fall under the following headings. (Some actual examples from government departments are given.)

- Financial performance (eg non-Exchequer income as a percentage of total income - National Engineering Laboratory)
- Volume of output (eg number of tests performed per period - Vehicle Inspectorate)
- Quality of service (eg error rate in the value of benefit payments - Employment Service)

- Efficiency (eg ratio of cost of support services to total cost - Laboratory of the Government Chemist)

Predicting business failure 5/95, 5/98

Altman's Z-score model can be used to try to predict the chance of business failure. It is calculated by taking several ratios and using them in a model to produce one final figure.

The following are ratios that might be used.

- ROCE
- Asset turnover
- Debt/equity
- Working capital/assets employed
- Retained profits/assets employed

The ratios are weighted and then compared with other companies.

- Companies that have failed in the past tended to have had low Z-scores and hence a company's low present Z-score may indicate the likelihood of failure in the future.
- Z-scores are not a perfect instrument for predicting failure but may be a useful guide.

Other studies of business failure include those of Beaver, Taffler and Argenti.

- *Beaver* conducted a study that shows that
  - The worst predictor of failure is current ratio
  - The best predictor of failure is cash flow/borrowings
- *Taffler's* approach is based on the following measures

- Earnings before tax/Current liabilities
- Current assets/Total liabilities
- Current liabilities/Total assets
- Sales/Total assets

- *Argenti* developed an A-score which judged likely failure by factors including
  - Autocratic chairman
  - Weak board
  - Poor financial control
  - Big project

Weaknesses of corporate failure models are as follows.

- They relate to the past, not taking account of macroeconomic changes
- They're limited by accounting concepts and conventions on which they're based
- The necessary accounting data may become available too late
- The measures used are subject to manipulation, if used by companies in setting objectives
- The definition of corporate failure is unclear, as various forms of rescue or restructuring are possible, short of liquidation

Exam focus. If a question were to require you to calculate an Altman Z score, or similar predictive measure, the formula would be given. Most important here is an understanding of the use and limitations of corporate failure models.

Financial difficulties may have the following *effects* on a business:

- *higher maintenance costs*, as plant replacement is deferred
- *reduced competitiveness*, as quality levels slip
- *loss of confidence* by customers, suppliers and lenders
- *recruiting problems*

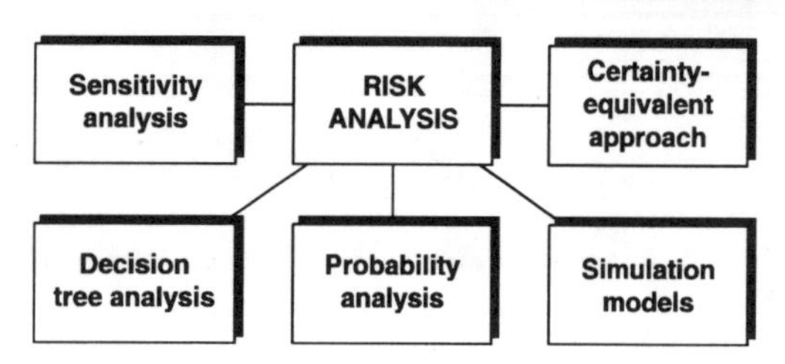

Risk analysis

5/96

The term risk applies where there are several possible outcomes and, on the basis of past relevant experience, probabilities can be applied to the various possible outcomes.

Projects are risky because future income and costs are subject to unforeseen changes.

The term *uncertainty* applies where there are several possible outcomes but there is little past experience to enable the probability of the possible outcome to be predicted.

Future cash flows cannot be predicted with certainty, and capital expenditure decisions might need to consider the risk or uncertainty involved.

Risk can be reflected by adjusting the cost of capital, and by techniques such as the following.

- *Sensitivity analysis,* such as estimating the extent to which cash flows can change for the worse before a project's NPV becomes negative
- *Probability analysis,* and the calculation of an expected value of the NPV (and also perhaps a standard deviation of the NPV)

- *Simulation* techniques and modelling, especially for large and complex projects
- Applying a *maximum payback period* as a cut-off time limit

> *Exam focus.* Where these topics are examined, it is likely to be in conjunction with other topics.

Sensitivity analysis

5/98

An approach to sensitivity analysis is as follows.

- Calculate the NPV of the project under alternative assumptions to determine how sensitive it is to changing conditions (eg changing selling price, sales volume or cost of capital)
- Use these calculations to see which are the critical (ie most sensitive) variables
- Review these variables to assess whether there is a strong possibility of a negative NPV

Sensitivity analysis indicates why a project might fail.

Weaknesses of the above approach are as follows.

- The method involves isolating each key variable, while management will probably be more interested in the combination of effects of changes in two or more key variables
- Sensitivity analysis does not examine probabilities of particular cost/revenue variations occurring

Certainty-equivalent approach

In the certainty-equivalent approach, expected future cash flows are multiplied by a factor to convert to riskless-equivalent amounts.

Eg, year 1, 2, 3 inward cash flows for a project might be reduced to certainty-equivalents by taking only 90%, 80% and 70% of them into account.

The method allows for different risk factors in each year, but the adjustments made are subjective.

Probability analysis

The steps of probability/expected values analysis are as follows.

- Estimate a probability distribution of expected cash flows
- Calculate an *expected* NPV

The analysis may be used to measure risk for example in the following ways.

- By calculating the probability of the worst possible outcome
- By calculating the probability that the project will fail to achieve a positive NPV
- By calculating the standard deviation of the NPV

If projects are mutually exclusive and carry different levels of risk, with the less risky project having a lower expected NPV, which project is selected will depend on management's attitude to risk.

- Risk-averse management will opt for less risky projects

- Other management may be prepared to risk the possibility of achieving a low NPV in the hope of achieving a high NPV

Simulation models

Simulation models (sometimes called 'Monte Carlo' simulations), which in practice are usually constructed using a computer, may overcome the following problems.

- Large or complex projects might require excessively complex decision trees
- Cash flows might be correlated over time (A project which is successful in early years is more likely to be successful in later years, with the result that the variation in NPV will not be reflected by a standard deviation calculation)

Simulation models are constructed by assigning a range of random number digits to each possible value of each uncertain variable, the range being selected so that when numbers are selected at random, the cash flows have the same probability of selection as indicated in their probability distribution.

> *Exam focus.* Where simulation is examined, you may be required to describe techniques and to assess their usefulness and limitations. Do not expect to be set a quantitative question on simulation.

Decision tree analysis

Decision trees can be useful where more than one variable affecting the NPV is uncertain, and using one involves two stages.

- Drawing the tree, to show all choices and outcomes

- Putting in the numbers: the probabilities, outcome values and expected values

Symbols for a decision tree

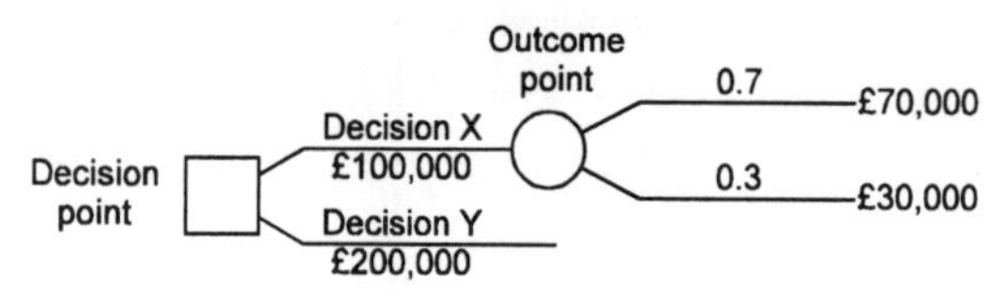

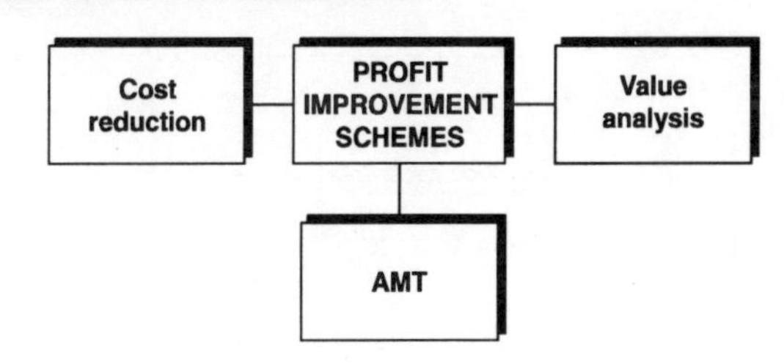

Profit improvement schemes

11/96

To enhance profit, it is important to be clear about the relationships: profit/volume and volume/cost.

Can prices be raised without a volume loss which more than compensates?

What is the likely effect of cost reductions on value and customer satisfaction?

Cost reduction

Be clear on the difference between:

- *Cost control*: the regulation of the costs of operating a business, and
- *Cost reduction*: a planned campaign to cut expenditure

The scope of a cost reduction programme should embrace the activities of the entire enterprise. It should have a long-term aim as well as short-term objectives.

In the long term, most costs, including 'fixed' costs, can be either reduced or avoided.

Value analysis

Value analysis is a radical examination of the factors affecting a product or service, to work out ways of achieving the specified purpose most economically.

Value engineering applies similar techniques to new products.

AMT

Advanced manufacturing technology (AMT) is associated with various developments in cost reduction which can be applied in a manufacturing environment.

- Just-in-time (JIT) manufacturing systems
- Manufacturing resource planning (MRP II)
- Numerical control (NC) technology
- Flexible manufacturing systems (FMS)

> *Exam focus.* You could be asked to discuss topics covered in this chapter in a part question. What is required here is an understanding of how net revenues may be increased by improving the performance of all activities in the business.

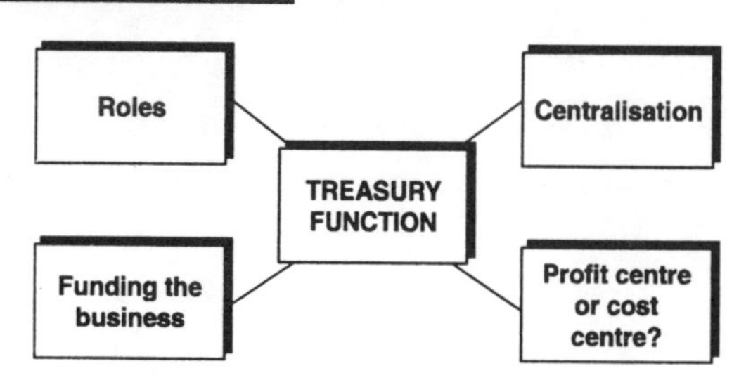

Roles 11/95, 11/98

The treasury department of a business enterprise has the following roles.

- Setting corporate financial objectives
- Management of the company's liquidity situation
- Funding management - eg term, cost, security
- Currency management
- Corporate finance - eg equity, acquisitions

Centralisation 11/95

Centralising the treasury function in a larger company may have a number of advantages, as follows.

- Centralised liquidity management avoids a mix of cash surpluses and overdrafts, saving interest costs
- Greater volumes of cash can be invested more profitably
- Larger borrowing may result in lower interest rates
- Netting of foreign currency transactions is possible
- Experts can more easily be hired

Profit centre or cost centre? 11/95

Setting up the treasury as a profit centre:

- Focuses treasury's attention on minimising costs of finance
- Will necessitate charging other divisions for treasury services
- Could promote risk-taking activity based upon treasury expectations of exchange movements (eg not hedging certain currencies)
- Could result in aggressive risk taking (eg buying currency not needed, buying or selling futures, and writing options). Such activities are difficult to control and can result in large losses

Setting up the treasury as a cost centre:

- Is less likely to lead to risk exposures
- Focuses treasury's attention on managing risks and reducing risk, not in risk-taking for profit
- Will be easier to control than a treasury run as a profit centre

Funding the business

The method of funding of current and fixed assets from long-term capital sources and from working capital (short-term) sources may be 'aggressive' or 'conservative' (see the diagram below).

A liquidity management policy somewhere between these extremes will probably achieve the best balance between risk and return.

Funding the business: alternative policies

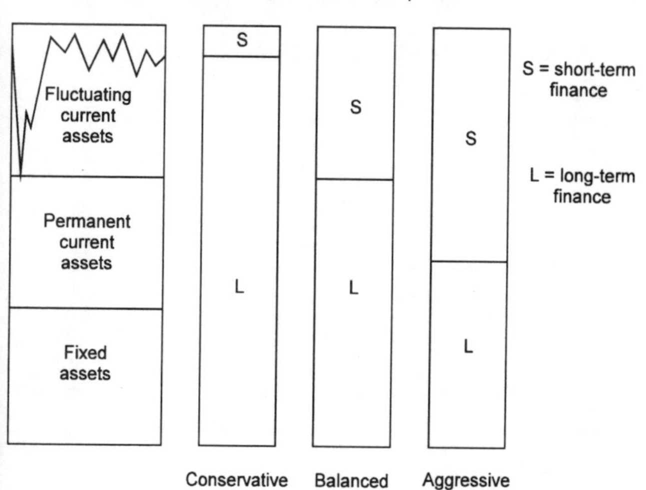

> *Exam focus.* The role of the treasury function is obviously central to questions where you are asked to put yourself in the role of treasurer. Alternatively, an essay question may cover the treasury function: important discussion points here are the benefits of having a separate treasury department and the profit centre v cost centre issue (both tested in 11/95).

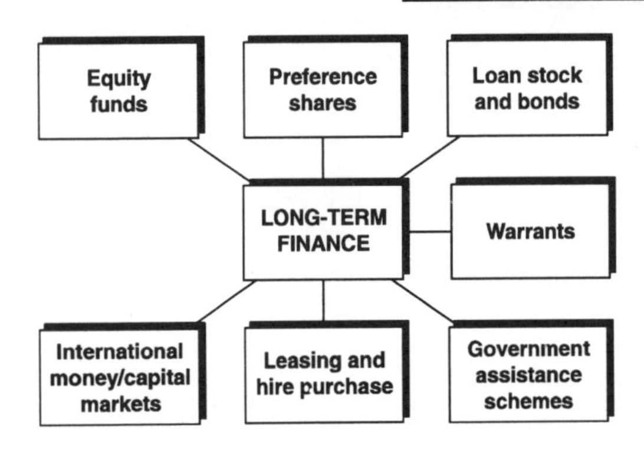

Long-term finance

5/95, 5/98

The following factors should be considered when raising long-term finance.

- Minimum/maximum loan limits
- Expense of raising funds
- Dilution of ownership
- Interference in decision making
- Security required
- Marketability - how easy will it be to persuade investors to invest?
- Signalling - how will the market react?
- Market liquidity - are funds available?

Companies, whether public or private, obtain long-term funds from a variety of sources.

- New issues of equity (ordinary) shares, preference shares, loan stock or bonds
- Retained profits - the most important source
- Bank borrowing (medium-term)

Cash from retained profits is the main source of long-term finance. (The profit retention/dividend decision is covered in Chapter 16.)

Equity funds

5/97, 5/98, 11/98

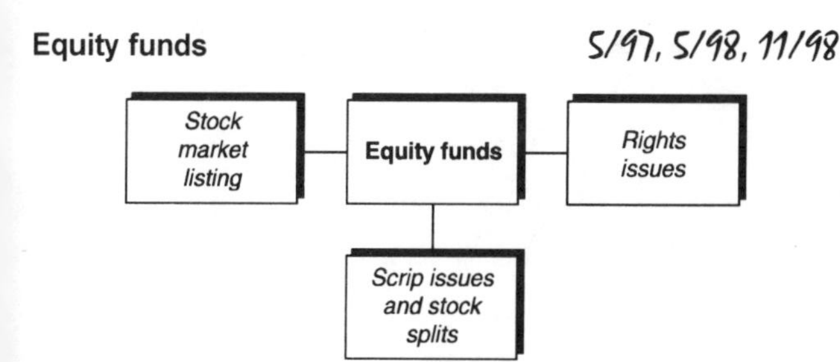

Stock market listing

In the UK, a company can bring its shares to the market for the first time (in a 'flotation') by the following methods.

- An offer for sale at either a set price, or (more rarely) by tender
- A placing, usually with institutional investors
- A prospectus issue
- A stock exchange introduction

A company that already has a stock market listing and that now wishes to issue new shares must either:

- Make the issue a *rights issue* (see below), whereby existing shareholders are invited to subscribe for all the new shares in a proportion to their existing shareholdings; or

- Obtain prior approval from shareholders for any other methods of share issue (for example, to finance a takeover with a share-for-share exchange as the method of compensation)

Not all companies seek a stock market quotation for their shares. The following are possible reasons for remaining as a private company.

- Insufficient size

- Insufficient past trading record

- No requirement for extra capital or rapid growth; adequate private funding

- To avoid burdens of stock market regulations

- To avoid pressures of stock market investors' expectations for earnings and dividend growth

- To retain ownership in the hands of a few individuals and thus avoid takeover threats

Small/medium-sized enterprises (SMEs) have wide access to borrowings, but have more difficulty in raising equity capital, for the following reasons.

- Small existing number of shareholders

- With no ready market for shares, investors will see their 'exit route' as restricted

- Limited information available for new investors

- Gearing may be high
- Enterprise may be non-diversified
- Outsiders may put lower value on the business than current owner/directors

Rights issues

A rights issue is an offer to existing shareholders to buy more shares usually at a price below the current share price.

Advantages of a rights issue are as follows.

- If shareholders exercise their rights, there is no dilution of their holding
- For shareholders, if they do not wish to or cannot afford to exercise their rights, they can sell them on the market
- The cost is lower than for a public issue
- Rights issues often boost the confidence of the market in the company
- Additional shares can increase marketability of the shares
- A rights issue can reduce gearing levels

Disadvantages of a rights issue are as follows.

- For the company, there is the problem of pricing the rights issue
- There is also the cost of having the issue underwritten or bearing the risk of an unsuccessful rights issue
- An unsuccessful rights issue will knock the confidence of the market in the company
- Share prices often drop after a rights issue

A company making a rights issue must set a price with the following characteristics.

- Low enough to secure shareholders' acceptance
- High enough to avoid excessive dilution of earnings per share (EPS)

If N is the number of rights required to buy 1 share, the value of a right is:

$$\frac{\text{Rights - on price} - \text{issue price}}{N + 1} = \frac{\text{Ex - rights price} - \text{issue price}}{N}$$

Formula given in Tables

The ex-rights price is:

$$\frac{1}{N+1}((N \times \text{rights - on price}) + \text{issue price})$$

Formula given in Tables

Note. In the CIMA formulae above, 'rights-on price' is another term for 'cum rights price'.

> *Exam focus.* In these Passcards, formulae included in the CIMA *Mathematical Tables* provided in the exam are indicated as above by the words *Formula given in Tables.*

Scrip issues and stock splits

Bonus issues (scrip issues), which are a way of increasing the number of shares in issue without raising any extra capital, by converting reserves into new share capital which is issued to existing shareholders.

Stock splits, which are another way of increasing the number of shares in issue without raising any extra capital, by dividing up existing shares into larger quantities with a smaller nominal value (eg a £1 share can be split into four shares of 25p each).

Scrip dividends, which involve the issue of new shares to existing shareholders as a dividend payment, in lieu of a cash dividend.

With *enhanced scrip dividends* - popular since 1993 - the share alternative offered is of greater value than the cash alternative.

Preference shares

Preference shares usually carry the following rights.

- A constant dividend expressed as % of nominal value
- Priority of dividends over ordinary shareholders
- Sometimes cumulative
- Priority over ordinary shareholders in a winding up (if stated in the Articles)

Why issue preference shares?

- Unlike interest payments on loans or debentures, the dividend payments can be missed in a poor year and preference shareholders cannot then appoint a receiver
- Compared with ordinary shares, there is no dilution of control since preference shares do not carry voting rights
- Unless they are redeemable, issuing preference shares will reduce gearing
- The company's borrowing powers will not be restricted, since there is no security against assets
- Preference shares are attractive to corporate investors as dividends received are not subject to corporation tax,

unlike interest received. *But*, for the issuing company, dividend payments are not tax-deductible, unlike interest payments

Loan stock and bonds 5/95, 11/97, 5/98, 11/98

'Bonds' is a term used to describe various forms of long-term debt.

Loan stock is long-term debt capital raised by a company for which interest is paid, usually half-yearly and commonly at a fixed rate of the nominal value of the stock.

Debentures are a form of loan stock, legally defined as written acknowledgement by a company of a debt, typically secured on company assets, usually given under seal and normally containing provisions about the payment of interest and eventual repayment of capital.

Loan stock/debentures might be redeemable or irredeemable. Redemption dates for redeemable stock might cover a period of time: then they must be redeemed by the latest specified date, but can be redeemed at the option of the company at any time after the earliest specified date.

Bonds or loans come in a variety of forms, for example as follows.

- *Floating rate debentures* are loans on which the coupon rate of interest can be varied at regular intervals, in line with changes in current market rates of interest.
- *Zero coupon bonds* are bonds issued at a large discount to their eventual redemption value, but on which no interest is paid. Investors obtain all their return from the capital gain on redemption.

- *Convertible loan stock* gives holders the right, if they wish, to convert their stock into shares at a predetermined rate at a future date
  - There may be a number of future dates for conversion, each with a different conversion rate for stock into shares
  - Convertible loan stock, because of the attraction of the option to convert into equity, will usually be issued at a lower rate of interest than current interest rates on 'ordinary' loan stock

Loans might be *secured* or *unsecured.*

- Mortgage loans are loans secured on property
- Bank loans might involve a fixed charge over certain fixed assets (eg property) and a floating charge over current assets (eg stocks and debtors) which will 'crystallise' if the bank wishes to use its security for repayment of an outstanding loan
- Companies might be able to issue *subordinated debt* or *junior debt* which is debt over which 'senior debt' takes priority
  - In the event of the company going into liquidation, holders of senior debt would be entitled to repayment out of realised assets of the company before holders of junior debt receive any payment
  - Being more risky for investors, junior debt carries a higher rate of interest

The term *mezzanine finance* describes loans, usually unsecured, which rank after secured debt but before equity in a winding up. Typically they carry interest up to around 3% above secured loans, and often carry an option to acquire equity to compensate for the riskiness of the debt.

Warrants

Share warrants are another form of security, often issued by companies as an 'add-on' to a new issue of loan stock to make the issue more attractive to investors.

Warrants give their holder the right to apply for new shares in the company at a fixed 'exercise' price at a future date or dates.

The price of a warrant should be at least as great as its *theoretical value.* The price will not of course be negative.

Theoretical value = excess of share price over exercise price × number of shares obtainable from 1 warrant

Excess of price of warrant over theoretical value = warrant conversion premium

Eg Share price 140 pence
Exercise price 100 pence
Price of warrant currently 50 pence, each entitled to 1 share

Theoretical value = (140 – 100) × 1 = 40 pence

Conversion premium = 50 – 40 = 10 pence

Government assistance schemes

> *Exam focus.* The Examiner recognises that the availability of government assistance is country-specific. What you need is awareness of the possibilities of such assistance and the major schemes operating in your country.

The freedom of European governments to offer cash grants and other forms of direct assistance is limited by European

Union policies designed to prevent the distortion of free market competition.

The following schemes are available in the UK.

- *The Enterprise Initiative*. Regional selective assistance and Regional Enterprise Grants
- *European Regional Development Funds (ERDF)*. Channelled through EU member governments
- *Loan Guarantee Scheme*

Tax incentives to UK investors in unquoted companies are provided by the *Enterprise Investment Scheme* and *venture capital trusts*.

Leasing and hire purchase 11/96, 5/98

Compared with outright purchase, all forms of leasing and hire purchase have the obvious advantage for the lessee/ purchaser that it is not necessary to pay for the asset in full.

An *operating lease* is a rental agreement, eg for a photocopying machine or a company car, by which the *lessor* remains responsible for servicing and maintenance of the asset.

- At the end of the lease period, the lessor might rent the equipment to someone else
- The lessee might avoid the risk of being stuck with obsolete equipment, and will not have to show the asset in the balance sheet (therefore, the gearing ratio will not increase)

A *finance lease* is an agreement covering most or all of the asset's expected useful life by which the *lessee* is responsible for servicing and maintenance of the asset.

- The lessor remains the legal owner of the asset, but might continue to lease the asset for only a nominal sum beyond the 'primary period' of the lease
- In substance, the lease is a financing arrangement which avoids the need to get, say, a bank loan to acquire an asset

Hire purchase (HP) is similar to finance leasing, except that ownership of the goods passes to the hire purchaser on payment of the final credit instalment.

- The purchaser can claim capital allowances on the purchase price of the asset - helpful if they can be used
- The interest element of payments is tax-allowable

The *lease or buy decision* involves choices between the following possibilities.

- Borrow cash and purchase outright
- Enter into lease agreement
- Enter into hire purchase agreement

There are two steps in arriving at a decision.

- Establish whether it is worth having the equipment by discounting the project's cash flows at a suitable cost of capital.
- If the equipment is worth having, compare the cash flows of purchasing, leasing and HP. The cash flows can be discounted at an after-tax cost of borrowing, and the financing method with the lowest PV of cost selected.

Note the following relevant cash flows.

- Borrow and purchase
  - Capital allowances (tax saving)
  - Repayment of loan
  - Tax saving on interest paid
- Finance lease (FA 91 rules)
  - Payments under lease
  - Tax saving on depreciation charged in the profit and loss account
  - Tax saving on interest charged in the profit and loss account

Exam focus. Unless the question says otherwise, you can assume that lease payments are fully tax-allowable, rather than use the above FA 91 rules. A *lessor* (leasing company) can take advantage of writing down allowances to set against taxable lease receipts. State your assumptions.

- Hire purchase
  - Payments under HP agreement
  - Capital allowances (tax saving)
  - Tax saving on interest charged in the profit and loss account

International money/capital markets

As well as seeking finance from domestic money and capital markets, companies are able to borrow funds:

- short/medium-term on the *eurocurrency* markets (international money markets), and
- long-term on the *eurobonds* and *euroequity* markets (international capital markets) - not for *smaller* companies

A company raising funds in these markets will be affected by changes in exchange rates.

> *Exam focus*. In exam answers, do not commit the error of associating these 'euro-' markets specifically with Europe. The euro- prefix really means 'denominated in another currency' here, and is not confined to European markets or currencies.
>
> Note also that it has nothing to do with the common European currency - the Euro.

Securitised debt, such as eurobonds, avoids the cost of intermediation and can be more flexible and quick to arrange than borrowing from a bank.

Eurocurrency lending may involve a *syndicate* of banks.

In a typical *multiple option facility* (MOF):

- A company may get a bank to put together a panel of banks to provide an amount in 'standby' loans over a period of, say, five years, perhaps at a rate related to LIBOR
- Another 'tender panel' of banks bids to provide loans
- The company can choose the lowest bid, or alternatively use the standby facility

Other markets available are those in *commercial paper* and *syndicated credits*.

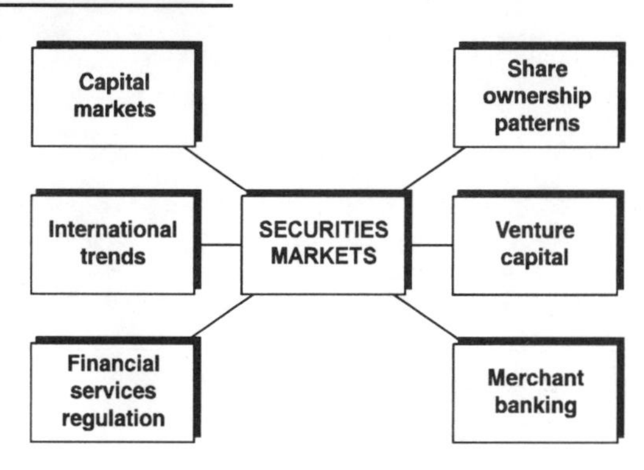

Capital markets

5/98

A *capital* market is a financial market in which long-term capital is bought or sold, or lent and borrowed. A stock market is a capital market for stocks and shares.

The role of a stock market for companies is:

- As a *primary market,* bringing companies and investors together through the issue of new securities, whereby
  - Investors put new long-term funds into a company and
  - A company can raise capital for investing in its business
- As a *secondary market* for existing stocks and shares, whereby
  - Investors can sell their stocks or shares if and when they wish to do so
  - Other investors can acquire existing stocks or shares in a company

A readily available market gives existing stocks and shares greater liquidity, which makes them much more attractive as investments.

Further functions of a stock market are as follows.

- To enable the owners of a company to realise some of their investment by their bringing a hitherto private company to the market
- To allow companies to take over other companies by issuing new shares as the purchase consideration. Listed companies can use their market status to finance expansion through acquisitions

The London Stock Exchange regulates:

- The *'main market'* of fully listed shares
- The second-tier *Alternative Investment Market (AIM)*

As well as forming the most important markets for shares in the UK, the London Stock Exchange is the capital market for UK government stocks (gilts).

> *Exam focus.* Past examiners' reports show that many students are unaware that not all plc's are listed on the Stock Exchange.

Methods of obtaining a stock market quotation are:

- *offer for sale by fixed price* to the general public
- *offer for sale* by tender
- *private placing* to a limited number of investors (usually institutions)
- *Stock Exchange introduction,* when shares are not made available

Share ownership patterns

Who owns the shares of a company can be important for management for the following reasons.

- Different shareholders prefer different dividend/retained earnings ratios
- Changes in shareholdings may explain share price movements
- Different shareholders have different preferences regarding risk and gearing
- Key shareholders may need to be identified in mounting a defence against an unwelcome takeover bid

In the UK, institutional investors now account for the majority of shares traded in the stock market, and divide into the following categories.

- Pension funds
- Insurance companies
- Investment trusts
- Unit trusts
- Venture capital organisations

Venture capital

5/96

Venture capital is money put into a risky new enterprise, which may all be lost if the enterprise fails.

- The investment is usually in return for an equity stake
- The investing company also often puts a director on the board, and might get involved in management as well

- Venture capital will usually be viewed as short-term from the investor's point of view, the aim being to provide an exit route for the venture capitalist such as taking the company to the AIM

Merchant banking 11/96, 11/97

Exam focus. This has been a frequently examined topic.

The activities of merchant banks (or 'investment banks') include:

- Management of and advice on the issue of shares and underwriting of issues, eg on
    - The need for other advisers
    - Pricing of issues, dividends
    - Stock Exchange listing requirements
    - Underwriting
- Taking wholesale deposits of funds, in domestic and foreign currencies
- Term lending to corporate borrowers
- Foreign exchange dealing
- Investment management, including for investment trusts, unit trusts, pension funds and charities
- Advice on takeovers, mergers and other matters
- Share registration
- Dealing in securities as a marketmaker or stockbroker, through a subsidiary company

Financial services regulation

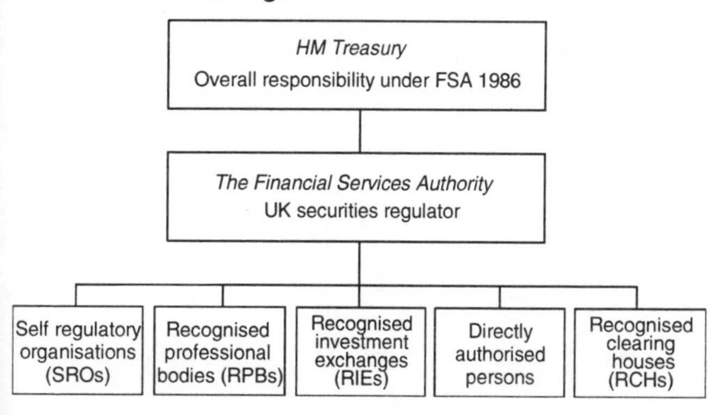

In the UK, the activities of the capital markets are regulated by the Financial Services Act 1986, which gives regulatory powers over the financial services industry, including capital markets, to the Financial Services Authority (FSA) (formerly the Securities and Investments Board (SIB)).

The FSA's regulatory powers are delegated to a number of Self-Regulatory Organisations (SROs).

The FSA's will also supervise banks in the future.

The main rules of the Stock Exchange are set out in the 'Yellow Book' - 'Admission of Securities to Listing'.

International trends

The following changes have affected capital markets in recent years.

- *Globalisation*: increasing international integration of the capital markets of individual countries
- *Securitisation of debt*: the issue of debt securities directly by companies, by-passing financial intermediaries
- *Risk assessment and risk management*: discussed later (Chapters 17 and 28-29)
- *Competition* among financial institutions has increased, helped by deregulation in many areas

Exam focus. You need to have knowledge of how a stock exchange operates and of the role of regulatory bodies.

The use of local examples from different countries is welcomed by the examiner.

Any questions requiring knowledge of UK institutions will be optional, not compulsory.

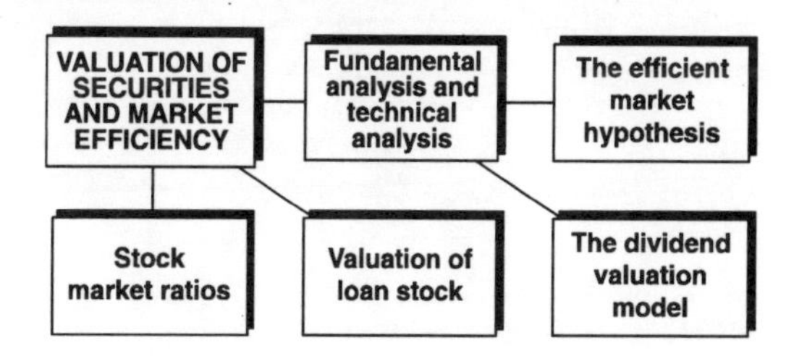

Fundamental analysis and technical analysis

There are two different views on the following questions.

- How are shares valued?
- Why do market values change?

These views are *fundamental analysis* and *technical analysis (or 'chartism')*.

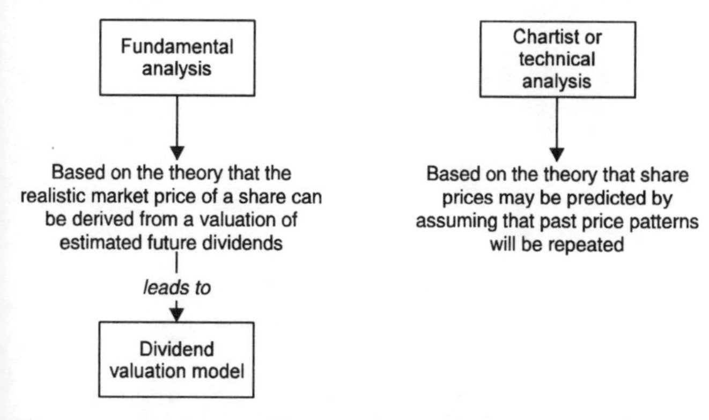

There are two types of investment analyst corresponding to these differing views.

Fundamental analysts study a company and its business, and attempt to uncover information about its current and future performance, in order to obtain an assessment of the value of the company's shares. The dividend valuation model, which stems from fundamental analysis theory, is summarised later in this Chapter.

Technical analysts (or chartists) study the share price movements in the past of a company's shares, and look for patterns or cycles in these price changes, for example upper or lower 'resistance levels' for prices. Breach of a resistance level, with the share price rising above or below it, would be interpreted as a significant shift in the pattern of price movements.

These analysts compete with each other to provide good and accurate information to investors.

- Fundamental research seeks to ensure that *all* relevant information is available
- Technical research ensures that information about past price changes is available, so that significant 'upswings' or 'downswings' in a share's price will quickly become known and the current share price will then move immediately and bring the trend or cyclical price movement to an end

The efficient market hypothesis 5/95

The efficient market hypothesis (EMH) is concerned with *information processing* efficiency in markets.

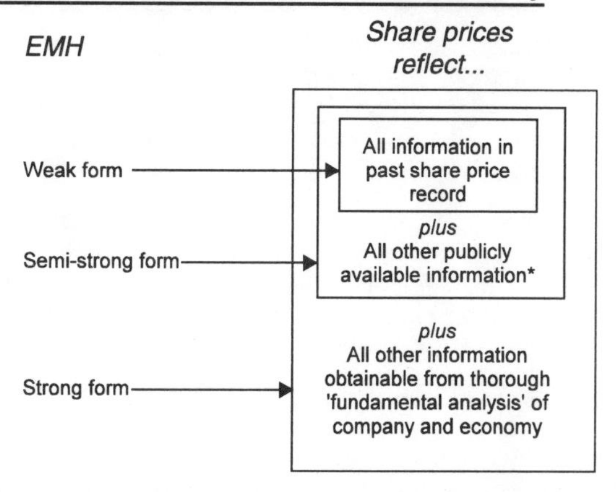

* such as announcements of earnings and dividends, earnings forecasts, announcements of mergers or takeovers and changes in accounting practice

An efficient market is one in which information is widely available to all investors, at a low cost, and all the available relevant information is already reflected in share prices and bond prices.

So, how 'efficient' is the stock market at processing information?

Also, is it possible for investors to 'out-guess' the market, making a profit by anticipating share price changes ahead of the rest of the market, and buying or selling shares to make money from their foresight?

- *Weak form* EMH is that share prices reflect all the information about companies in the record of past share prices

- *Semi-strong form* EMH is that share prices reflect not just all information in the record of past share prices, but also all publicly available information, such as announcements of earnings and dividends, earnings forecasts, takeover announcements and changes in accounting practice

- *Strong form* EMH is that share prices reflect not just all information in the record of past share prices and all publicly available information, but also *all* information obtainable from very thorough 'fundamental analysis' of companies and the economy

If the market has strong form efficiency, an investor cannot, except by luck, to 'out-guess' the market and make profits by buying and selling shares with better 'insider knowledge' than others about how share prices will change. The market value of a share will reflect the intrinsic value of that share.

Whatever form of efficiency the markets show,

- Current share prices reflect all the information that the market 'uses'

- Share prices change only when new information becomes available

The relationship between the EMH, fundamental analysis and chartism can be summarised as follows.

- *Weak form EMH:* if true, *chartists* cannot gain

- *Semi-strong form EMH:* if true, *fundamental analysts* cannot gain

- *Strong form EMH:* if true, even *insiders* cannot gain

The dividend valuation model 5/95, 11/97, 5/98

A well established theory of share values is that an equilibrium price for any share (or bond) on a stock market is:

- The future expected stream of income from the security
- Discounted at a suitable cost of capital

Equilibrium market price is thus a present value of a future expected income stream.

The annual income stream for a share is the expected dividend every year in perpetuity.

If an investor *sells* his shares in the future, the price he will get is the PV of the expected future dividend stream in perpetuity, and so (assuming insignificant transaction costs) we can ignore expected capital gains on share sales, and use dividend streams to value shares.

The PV of £1 per annum in perpetuity from year 1 onwards is £1/r, and so if there is no expected dividend growth, the ex div market value per share (p_0) will be:

$$p_0 \text{ (or MV ex div)} = \frac{d}{r}$$

where d is the annual dividend (in perpetuity)
r is the cost of share capital, which is the return expected by the shareholders

The cost of equity capital *might* be estimated using the Capital Asset Pricing Model (covered in Chapter 15).

If there is expected *dividend growth* of g per annum, with g as a proportion or percentage:

$$p_0 = \frac{d_1}{(r - g)}$$

where d_1 is next year's (year 1's) dividend.

(Note that $d_1 = d_0(1+g)$, where d_0 is the current year's dividend.)

The estimated growth rate g might be:

- Based on historical growth rates in the past, projected into the future, or
- Based on the formula: $g = bR$

where b is the proportion of annual earnings that are retained in the business, and

R is the expected annual return (%) on these re-invested profits.

Both b and R are assumed to be constant each year.

Valuation of loan stock

For irredeemable loan stock or debentures, the ex-interest market value (p_0) is given by the following.

$$p_0 \text{ (or MV ex int)} = \frac{i}{r}$$

where i is the annual interest payment ('coupon')
r is the return required by the investors

For redeemable loan stock, the market value is the discounted present value of future interest receivable *plus* the discounted present value of the redemption payment.

Stock market ratios

11/95

Current market prices for securities enable investors:

- To measure and compare the returns on various stock market investments
- To relate the amount of returns that are being earned to the market value of the investments

The stock market ratios described below are used to measure and compare equity returns.

Earnings per share (EPS) are the after-tax profits available for *ordinary* shareholders *after* any extraordinary items, divided by the number of ordinary shares in issue and ranking for dividend.

EPS is a measure of profit performance, which can be used to judge progress (growth) from one year to the next.

> *Exam focus.* The Examiner has commented that many candidates do not know how to calculate earnings per share correctly. Make sure that you do!

If a company *issues new shares* for cash at a current market price after x months of the year, the EPS for the year is calculated by adjusting the number of shares in issue during the current year to a weighted amount. Suppose that the new shares are issued after three months of the year.

	Number of shares in issue	*Proportion of year*	*Weighting*
Before the new issue	X	3/12	0.25X
After the new issue	Y	9/12	0.75Y
Weighted number of shares			0.25X + 0.75Y

The EPS is calculated by dividing total earnings by this weighted number of shares, thus giving a direct comparison with the previous year's EPS.

Rights issues involve a new issue of shares at a price below their market value. Shares after the rights issue cannot therefore be compared directly with shares before the issue, because they have different values and (implicitly) different 'earning power'.

The EPS for the *previous* year is multiplied by the fraction:

$$\frac{\text{Theoretical ex - rights price}}{\text{Market price on last day of quotation cum rights}}$$

To obtain an EPS for the *current* year, the number of shares in issue is adjusted to arrive at an appropriate weighted total.

A Multiply the number of shares *before* the rights issue by:

- The fraction of the year before the date of issue, and
- By the fraction

$$\frac{\text{Market price on last day of quotation cum rights}}{\text{Theoretical ex - rights price}}$$

B Multiply the number of shares *after* the rights issue by the fraction of the year after the date of issue

C Add the figure in A to the figure in B to arrive at a total number of shares

D Divide total earnings by this weighted total of shares in C

A *fully diluted EPS* (FDEPS) can be measured where the company has issued securities that might be converted into ordinary shares at some future date, such as convertible loan stock, share warrants or share options.

Since the FDEPS will usually be less than the EPS, it is a 'watered down' or 'diluted' earnings figure, giving investors an appreciation of by how much EPS might be affected if and when the options, warrants or conversion rights are exercised.

Total earnings are increased by:

- The savings in interest (net of tax) from the conversion of loan stock into shares
- The addition to profits (net of tax) from investing the cash obtained from the exercise of share options or warrants (estimated on the assumption that the cash is invested in 2½% Consolidated Stock at their market price on the first day of the period)

$$\text{FDEPS} = \frac{\text{Adjusted earnings}}{\text{Maximum number of ordinary shares}}$$

> *Exam focus.* Detailed knowledge of, for example, the implications of unrecovered ACT on EPS calculations (ie whether to use the nil or net basis) will not be examined in the SFM paper. Questions will always assume that the company has no unrecoverable ACT.
>
> However, the calculation of diluted EPS needs to be understood.

The *P/E ratio* for a share is the ratio of its market price to its EPS. P/E ratios can be used:

- To compare the market values of shares in different companies
- To assess the stock market's expectations of future earnings growth in a company

Note the following points.

- A well established listed company is likely to have a higher P/E ratio than a company with a recent stock market listing, since it is more 'well known' and perceived as less risky
- A bigger company is possibly likely to have a higher P/E ratio than a smaller company in the same industry and

with the same growth expectations. A larger size implies a smaller investment risk

- Companies in low-risk industries or high-growth industries will have higher P/E ratios than companies in high-risk or low-growth industries
- Individual companies which are expected to achieve a high EPS growth into the future will have a higher P/E ratio than comparable companies with low EPS growth expectations
- Dividend policy can affect P/E ratios, with investors *perhaps* willing to pay more for shares in a company with a policy of paying high dividends

Dividend yield is the gross dividend per share as a percentage of the share's market value. In the financial press, the dividend is grossed up (by adding the appropriate tax credit) to calculate the yield. This makes dividend yield comparable with interest yields on loan stock.

A low dividend yield is not necessarily bad news: it could be that the company retains a high proportion of earnings for reinvestment.

Earnings yield is most commonly calculated as:

$$\frac{\text{Grossed up EPS calculated on net basis *}}{\text{Share price}} \times 100$$

(* Net basis: earnings calculated by deducting the actual taxation charge, as required by SSAP3.)

Earnings yield will be important to investors who are more concerned with capital growth than dividends.

Dividend cover measures the ratio of distributable profits per share (the maximum possible equity dividend) to the actual ordinary dividends, as:

$$\frac{\text{EPS}}{\text{Net dividend}}$$

Dividend cover indicates how safe the dividend is, or the extent to which profits are being retained.

Interest yield on loan stock equals:

$$\frac{\text{Gross interest}}{\text{Market value}} \times 100\%$$

Eg £100 loan stock in ABC plc is currently priced at £82½. The *coupon* is 7%.

$$\text{Interest yield} = \frac{100 \times 7\%}{82.5} \times 100\% = 8.48\%$$

Exam focus. Remember that choice and interpretation of ratios is as important as their correct calculation in the Paper 13 exam.

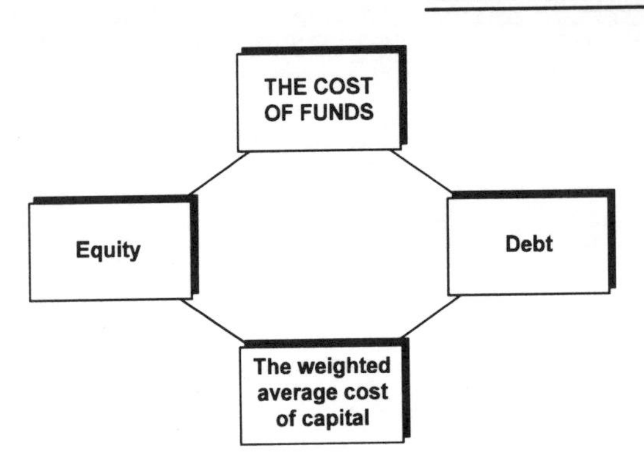

The cost of funds

The cost of capital is the rate of return that the enterprise must pay to satisfy the providers of funds.

Cash flows paid by the company = Cash flows received by the investor

Therefore the cost of capital for the company can be found using the same formulae as the return on shares to the investor.

Equity

The cost of equity is the return that ordinary shareholders expect to receive from their investment. It is appropriate to measure this in terms of either:

- The net dividend that the company pays (dividend valuation model of the cost of equity), or
- The net dividend that the company pays plus any capital gain on the share in a one year time span (capital asset pricing model valuation of the cost of equity)

The *dividend valuation model with no dividend growth* gives a cost of equity r as follows.

$$r = \frac{d_1}{p_0}$$

where d_1 is the annual net dividend
p_0 is the ex div market price of the share

The *dividend valuation model with dividend growth* of g per annum expected, with g expressed as a proportion, gives us the following.

$$r = \frac{d_1}{p_0} + g$$

Formula given in Tables

With either dividend valuation model, it should be clear that r, d_1 and p_0 are closely interrelated. If r increases but d_1 is unchanged, p_0 will fall. If d_1 rises but r is unchanged, p_0 will rise, and so on.

In the *capital asset pricing model* (CAPM), the expected return on a share (or cost of equity) $E(r_j)$ is stated in the CAPM formula as follows.

$$E(r_j) = r_f + [E(r_m) - r_f]\ \beta_j$$

Formula given in Tables

where r_f is the risk-free rate of return
$E(r_m)$ is the expected market rate of return
β_j is the beta factor of the company's equity shares

The CAPM and beta factors are covered in more detail in Chapter 15.

Debt

The cost of loan stock, debentures or bank loans is the return which the company must provide its lenders. In the following formula, r is the cost of debt.

For *irredeemable debt* (or preference shares):

$$i = \frac{i(1-T)}{p_0}$$

where i is the interest (or preference dividend) received
T is the rate of tax
p_0 is the ex interest (or ex div) market value of loan stock (or preference shares)

For *redeemable debt,* the cost of debt is given by the internal rate of return of the following cash flows (assuming that the tax saving is simultaneous with the relevant interest payment).

Year	*Item*	*Cash flow*
	£	
0	Market value of loan	p_0
1 to n	Annual interest until redemption of loan in year n	$i(1-T)$ per annum
n	Redemption value of loan	RV

Depending on the circumstances, the tax saving might instead come one year later, in years 2 to (n + 1).

You should understand the logic for calculating the cost of *convertible securities.* The cost of fixed interest securities convertible into ordinary shares is found as follows, assuming tax savings are simultaneous with interest payments and assuming that conversion will take place.

$$p_0 = \frac{I(1-T)}{(1+r)} + \frac{I(1-T)}{(1+r)^2} + \ldots + \frac{I(1-T)}{(1+r)^n} + \left(\frac{V_n \times C}{(1+r)^n}\right)$$

where p_0 is the current market price of the convertible security, convertible in year n, after paying the current year's interest

- I is the annual interest payment
- T is the rate of corporation tax
- r is the cost of capital of the convertible security holders
- V_n is the market value of an ordinary share in year n
- C is the conversion ratio, that is the number of shares into which the security is convertible

The cost of capital, r, would be calculated by finding the IRR which equates p_0 with the present value of the future cash flows.

If the cost of capital found by treating the convertibles as non-convertible debentures is higher, that higher cost should be used.

> *Exam focus.* In practice, factors influencing the cost of convertible debentures are various, including expected future share prices, the expected proportion of holders who will convert and the dates of expected conversion, as well as the market value of debentures and interest rates. In exam questions, examples given must inevitably be simplified.

The weighted average cost of capital 5/98, 11/98

The *weighted average cost of capital* (WACC) of a company's capital structure is the average of the cost of its equity, preference shares and various forms of permanent/long-term loans, weighted to allow for the market value of each of these capital items.

A general formula giving the weighted average cost of capital or WACC for a company financed by debt and equity is:

$$r_D\,(1 - T_C)\left(\frac{D}{E + D}\right) + r_E\left(\frac{E}{E + D}\right)$$

Formula given in Tables

where r_E is the cost of equity
r_D is the cost of debt
E is the market value of equity in the firm
D is the market value of debt in the firm
T_C is the marginal rate of taxation

> *Exam focus.* Note that this is the only formula in the CIMA *Mathematical Tables* provided in the exam where the cost of equity is shown as r_E. Elsewhere in the *Cost of capital* section of the tables, r is used to signify the cost of equity.

Note that the market value of the company (E + D) is maximised when the WACC is minimised.

The formula above works only for irredeemable debt.

> *Exam focus.* If you are given a pre-tax cost of debt and no details about the nature of the debt, assume that it is irredeemable.
>
> If you need to calculate a WACC given redeemable debt, then calculate the after-tax cost of debt and substitute into the formula instead of $r_D(1 - T_C)$.

A company's WACC can be regarded as its opportunity cost of capital/marginal cost of capital, and this cost of capital can be used to evaluate the company's investment projects with discounted cash flow (DCF) analysis, *if the following conditions 1-3 apply.*

- 1: the project is small relative to the size of the company
- 2: the company will maintain its existing capital structure in the long run (ie same *financial risk*)
- 3: the project has the same degree of systematic (business) risk - defined in Chapter 15 - as the company has now

An alternative arrangement of the above WACC formula is shown in the summary diagram below.

Use of WACC in project appraisal

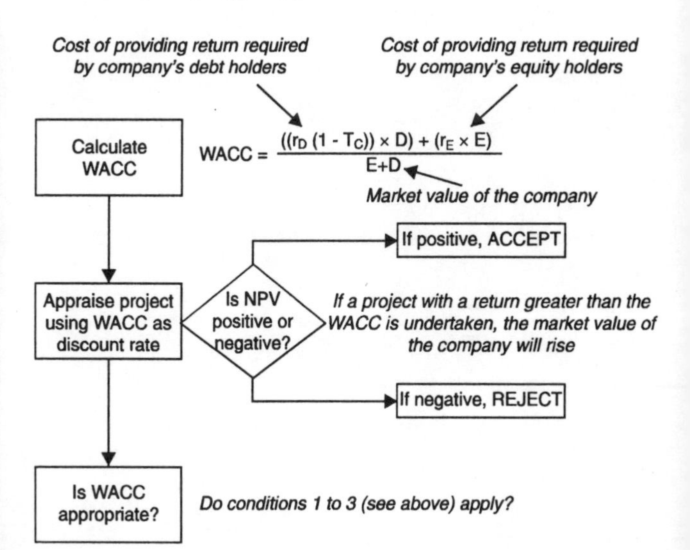

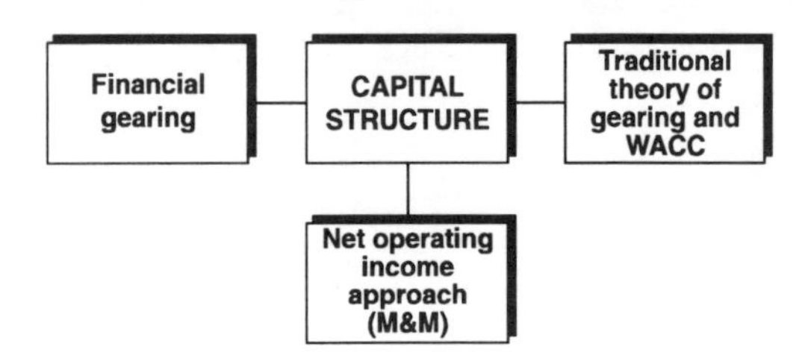

Financial gearing

11/95

Definition of *financial gearing*: the increased variability of earnings that results from including debt finance in the capital structure of a company. (Gearing is called 'leverage' in North America.)

There are two main theories about the relationship between a company's level of financial gearing and its cost of capital.

Both theories are concerned with whether there is an 'ideal' level of financial gearing for a company. Any such level will be one at which the company's weighted average cost of capital (WACC) is minimised.

Both theories agree that:

- The cost of equity is higher than the cost of debt (because of the higher investment risk)
- The cost of equity will increase as a company's level of financial gearing rises, because of the higher financial risk as gearing increases

Traditional theory of gearing and WACC

The traditional theory is that as a company's gearing increases above zero, WACC will:

- Fall initially, because of the higher proportion of lower-cost debt capital in the firm's capital structure, but
- Eventually increase when gearing gets above a certain level, because the rising cost of equity offsets the higher proportion of low cost debt

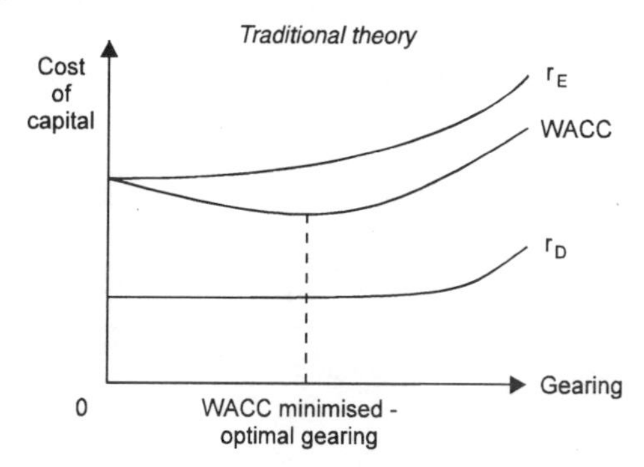

Net operating income approach (M&M)

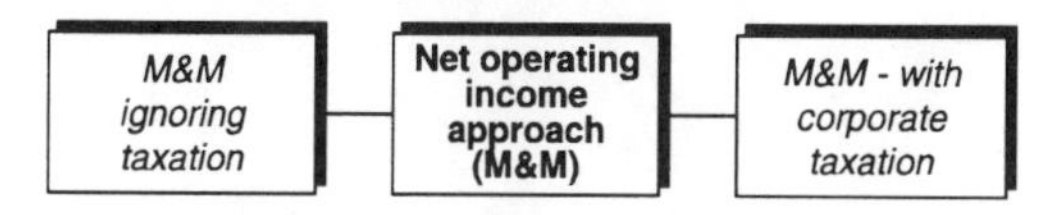

An alternative theory of gearing, the net operating income approach, was supported by the US academics Modigliani and Miller (M&M).

M&M's assumptions:

- Investors are rational
- Information is freely available
- There are no transaction costs

- Debt is risk-free
- Investors are indifferent between corporate and personal borrowing

M&M argued that if we ignored corporate taxes (and tax relief for companies on interest, which reduces the cost of debt capital) the cost of equity would rise as gearing rises so as to *offset exactly* the benefits of the increasing proportion of lower-cost debt capital.

The net result is that the WACC is the same at all levels of gearing, ie gearing is irrelevant to project valuation.

M&M later modified their theory to allow for corporate taxes (and tax relief on interest charges), concluding that because of the tax shield for debt interest, a company's WACC will continue to fall as gearing rises, until it is minimised at the level where the company is financed entirely by debt capital.

This is because *arbitrage* by investors (buying and selling shares and debt capital to profit from different market prices for the securities of different companies) would keep the WACC constant.

Exam focus. Be prepared to explain in the exam how arbitrage works.

M & M - ignoring taxation

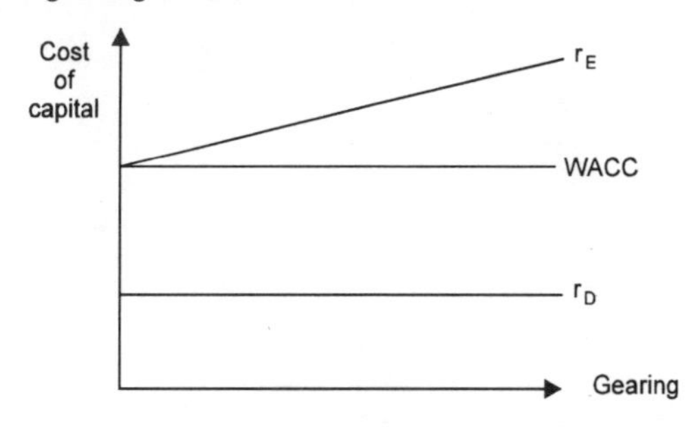

The cost of equity is higher in a geared company than in an equivalent ungeared company, by a measurable amount.

$$r_E = r + \left[(r - r_D) \times \frac{D}{E}\right]$$

where r_E is the cost of equity in a geared company
r is the cost of equity in an ungeared company
r_D is the cost of debt capital
D is the market value of the debt capital (irredeemable debt) in the geared company
E is the market value of the equity in the geared company

Since the WACC is the same in companies regardless of gearing level, the total market value will be the same for companies that are identical in every respect except for their gearing level.

$$V_u = V_g$$

where V_u is the market value of an all equity company, and V_g (= E + D) is the total market value of the identical geared company.

M & M - with corporate taxation

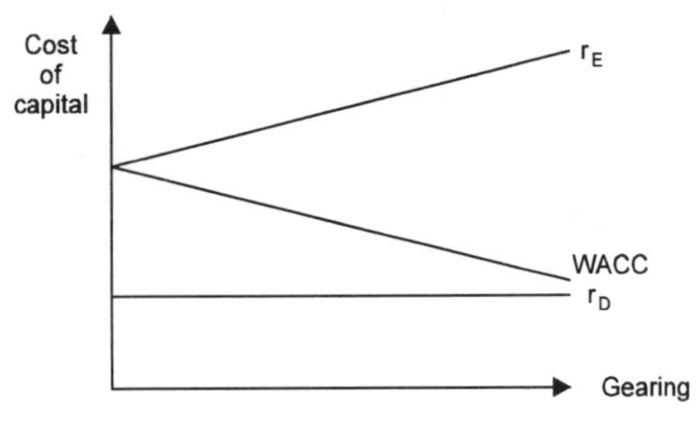

The cost of equity is still higher in a geared company than in an ungeared company, but by an amount which must be adjusted (by $(1 - T_C)$) to allow for tax relief on debt interest, where T_C is the rate of corporation tax expressed as a decimal (eg 0.3 for 30% tax).

$$r_E = r + (1 - T_C)\left[(r - r_D) \times \frac{D}{E}\right]$$

From the above formula, it is possible to derive the following formula for the WACC of a geared company:

$$r(1 - T^*L)$$

Formula given in Tables

where L is equivalent to $\frac{D}{E+D}$

T^* is the tax saving due to interest payments, usually equal to the corporation tax rate

The WACC in a geared company will be lower than the WACC in an ungeared company by a measurable amount. WACC will fall as gearing increases.

$$WACC_g = WACC_u \times \frac{V_u}{V_g}$$

The total value (equity plus debt capital) of a geared company (V_g) will *exceed* the value of an identical ungeared company (V_u), by an amount DT_C.

$$V_g = V_u + DT_C$$

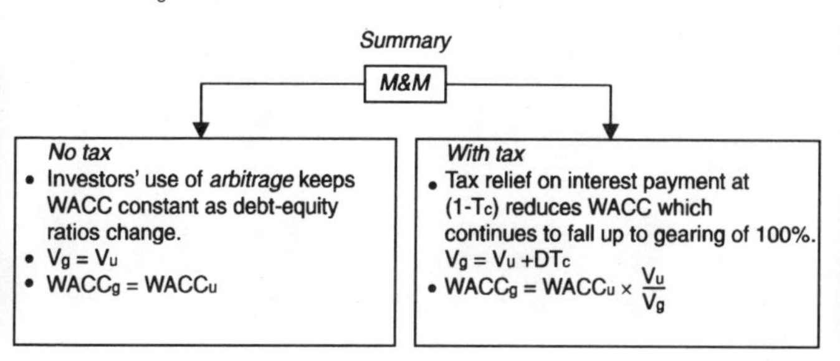

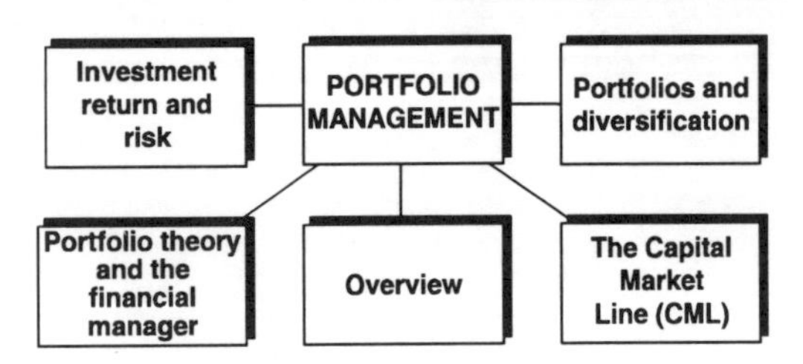

Investment return and risk

5/96

Risk is measured as the variability (or standard deviation) of returns.

Investors buy stocks and shares to make a *return*. Return can be measured by the capital gain on the security, if it goes up in price, plus any dividend or interest received.

$$\text{Return on share in period} = \frac{\text{Dividend + capital gain in the period}}{\text{Share price at start of period}}$$

Companies invest in projects, and make a return from the cash inflows from the projects.

Returns might be higher or lower than expected, and this variability in returns is the cause of investment risk. Some investments are more risky than others, which means that their returns are likely to be more variable and 'erratic'.

Investments in debt capital are less risky than investments in equity shares, because returns are more certain and stable. However, much debt capital has some risk, since market prices can go up or down and this causes capital gains or losses.

Some short-term debt capital is virtually risk-free, such as Treasury bills and eligible bank bills in the UK.

An investor will be willing to accept more risk for a bigger return. His willingness to trade off risk and return can be described by an indifference curve.

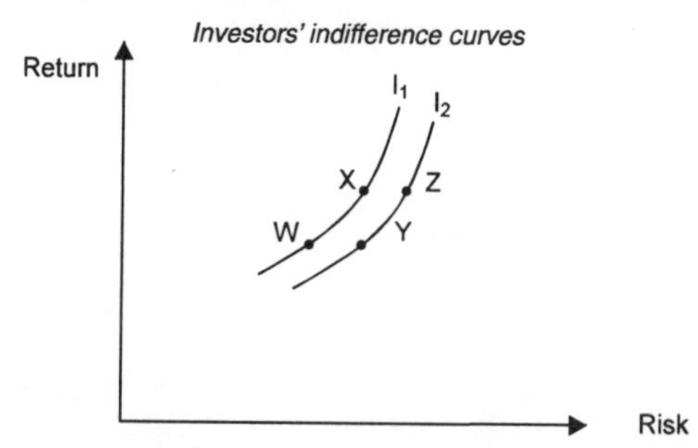

The investor would be indifferent about choosing any investment or portfolio of investments that lie on the same indifference curve.

- W and X in the diagram above have equal merit. The lower return on W is compensated by the lower risk
- Y and Z have equal merit. The lower return on Y is compensated by the lower risk
- W or X will be preferred to Y or Z, on the basis of *mean-variance efficiency*, because they lie on the indifference curve I_1 that offers a higher return for the same risk or equal return for a lower risk than investments on indifference curve I_2

Portfolios and diversification

5/96, 11/97

Investors can reduce their investment risk by diversifying, and building up a portfolio of investments.

The expected return $\bar{r}_p$ of a two-asset portfolio will be given by:

$$\bar{r}_p = x\bar{r}_a + (1-x)\,\bar{r}_b$$

where x is the proportion of investment A in the portfolio
$\bar{r}_a, \bar{r}_b$ are the expected returns of investments A and B

Some portfolios will offer higher returns or less risk than others. If a graph could plot, for every possible portfolio of securities, the return and associated risk of the portfolio, the dots representing each portfolio would form a roughly oval-shaped cluster on the graph.

Portfolio return and risk: the efficient frontier

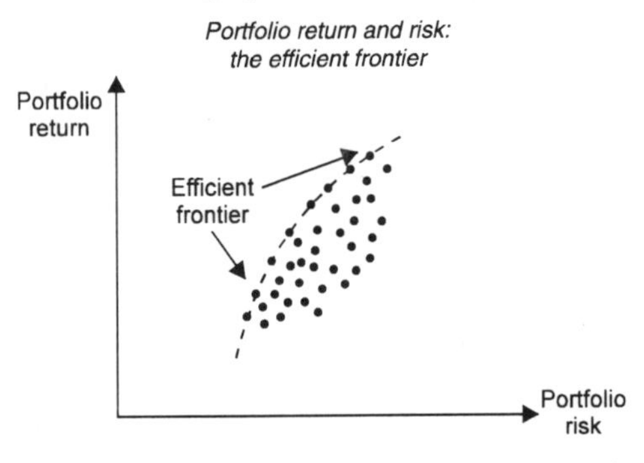

Some portfolios would offer *either* a higher return *or* lower risk in comparison with any other individual portfolio. These 'efficient' portfolios lie along the *efficient frontier*.

An investor should select the portfolio that is on the efficient frontier and touches one of his indifference curves at a tangent, because this will give him an optimal feasible combination of return and risk to suit his preferences. This is portfolio M on the graph below.

The optimum portfolio

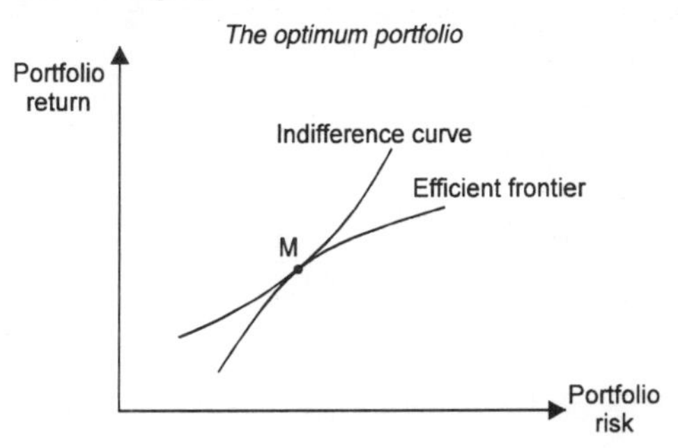

Portfolio M is likely to be the portfolio preferred by all risk-averse investors.

The Capital Market Line (CML)

So far, the analysis has ignored risk-free investments (such as government stocks).

The Capital Market Line

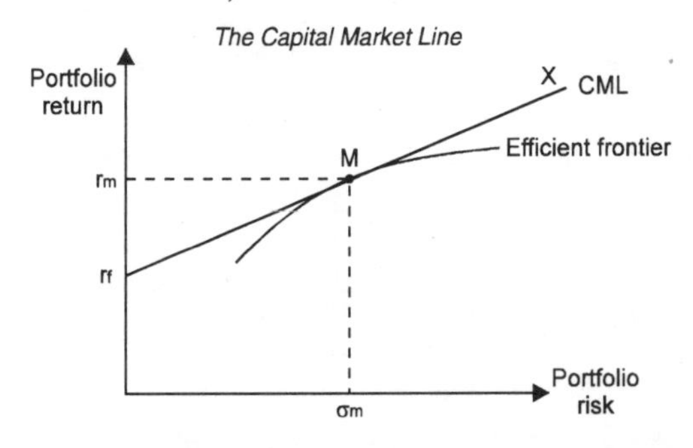

In the diagram above, an investor can choose risky investments in portfolio M or risk-free investments, whose return is r_f. The market return is r_m.

- He could combine portfolio M with risk-free investments, to create a portfolio that would be between r_f and M on the line in the graph above
- If he could borrow at a risk-free rate r_f and invest in more of portfolio M with the borrowed funds, he could create a portfolio that would lie between M and X on the line in the graph above

If we consider investors as a whole rather than individual investors:

- Since all investors would wish ideally to hold portfolio M, and
- All shares quoted on a stock exchange must be held by investors, then
- All shares quoted on a stock exchange will be in the 'ideal' portfolio M

The line ($r_f \rightarrow M \rightarrow X$) in the graph above is a new 'efficient frontier' of investments for all investors, and this is called the Capital Market Line.

It is in the nature of the stock market that an investor might succeed in building up a portfolio whose return and risk characteristics would make it lie above the CML. Any such portfolio would be regarded as super-efficient.

Portfolios can also be built up with return and risk characteristics that would put it below the CML. These portfolios are inefficient, and could be improved by altering the composition of the portfolio.

The slope of the CML can be measured as $\frac{r_m - r_f}{\sigma_m}$

The equation for the expected return for any portfolio on the CML is $r_f + \left(\frac{r_m - r_f}{\sigma_m}\right)\sigma_p$

where σ_p is the risk (standard deviation of return) of the particular portfolio.

A high level of diversification leads to the investor holding the *market portfolio*, with investments reflecting the risk and return characteristics of all shares in the market.

It has been shown that in practice only 10 to 12 or so diverse shares are needed to reach this position, at which portfolio risk σ_p equals market risk σ_m.

Overview

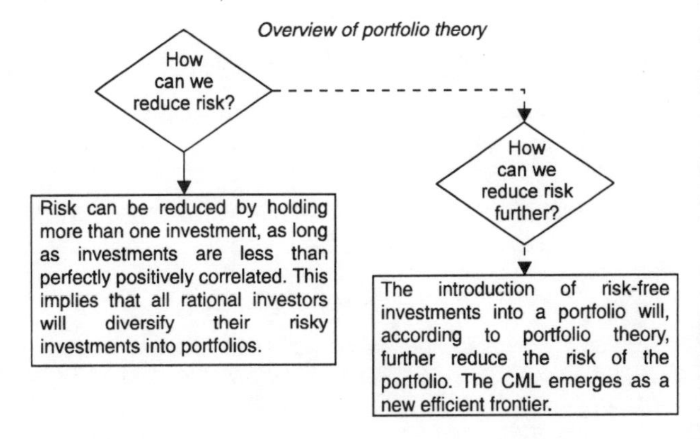

Portfolio theory and the financial manager

Can portfolio theory be applied to a company choosing projects to invest in? Diversification has advantages, but there are the following limitations.

- Estimating risk and correlations between project returns is problematic
- Limited knowledge of shareholders' preferences between risk and return will make it difficult to reflect these preferences in decision-making
- With their job security to consider, managers may be more risk-averse than the theory would dictate (the 'agency problem')
- Projects may not divide to allow for diversification
- The theory does not take account of possible economies of scale from making a larger investment in a single project

Exam focus. It is important that you appreciate the issues to do with using portfolio theory in practice.

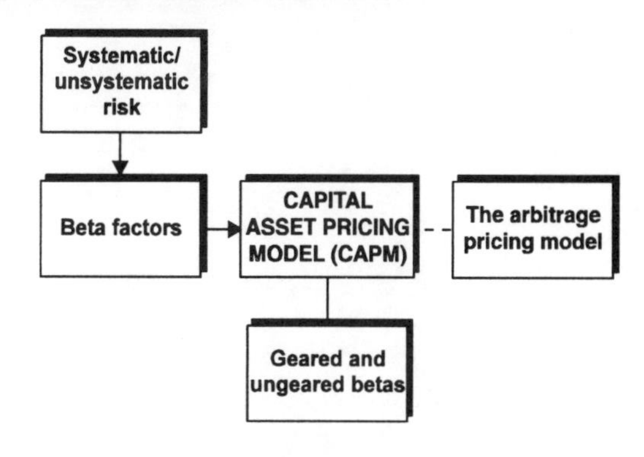

Systematic/unsystematic risk

5/95

The returns obtained from an individual security are variable, and the reasons for variations could be:

- 1: factors unique to the company itself or even a single project that the company is undertaking
- 2: factors unique to the company's industry
- 3: economic factors affecting the country as a whole

Factors of types 1 and 2 are risk items that an investor can eliminate by diversifying. Factor type 3 is unavoidable, non-diversifiable risk, which is greater for some projects or companies than for others.

Risk that can be diversified away (and variations in returns which tend to cancel themselves out over time) is called *unsystematic risk.* Non-diversifiable risk is called *systematic risk* (or market risk).

Beta factors

The systematic risk of an individual company's shares might be higher or lower than the average risk for the market as a whole. (Similarly, the systematic risk for some projects is greater or less than for others.)

The relationship between an individual security's risk and the average market risk can be measured as a beta factor or β.

Mathematically, the beta factor (β_i) of security i can be expressed in terms of:

- $Cov_{i,m}$ - the covariance of returns on the security with the market return, and
- σ_m^2 - the variance of market returns

$$\beta_i = \frac{Cov_{i,m}}{\sigma_m^2}$$

Formula given in Tables

A security's beta factor can be estimated by comparing returns on the security (eg an equity share) and average market returns for each time period (each month, say) over a long period of time. Linear regression techniques can be used.

- The market as a whole has a $\beta = 1$
- A risk-free security has a $\beta = 0$
- A security with a $\beta < 1$ has non-diversifiable risk below the market average
- A security with a $\beta > 1$ has non-diversifiable risk above the market average

Exam focus. You will not be expected to calculate beta factors from raw data.

By combining securities into a portfolio, risk is reduced but there will be some non-diversifiable risk.

The beta factor for a portfolio can be measured as the weighted average of the beta factors of individual securities in the portfolio, with weightings based on the *market values* of the securities in the portfolio.

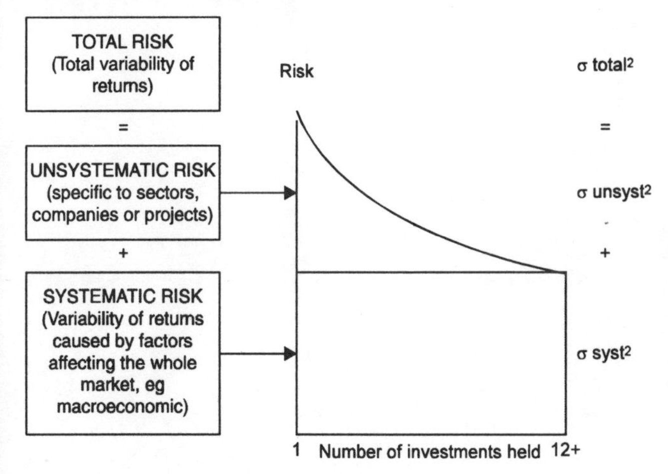

Note the following points.

- The extent to which investments are subject to systematic risk is measured by β factors
- Rational investors will diversify fully and will therefore be subject only to systematic risk
- β factors can be found for any project or investment whose returns can be compared with market returns

Capital Asset Pricing Model (CAPM) 5/96, 11/97, 11/98

The higher the β for a security (or portfolio, or project) the greater the return an investor will want from it.

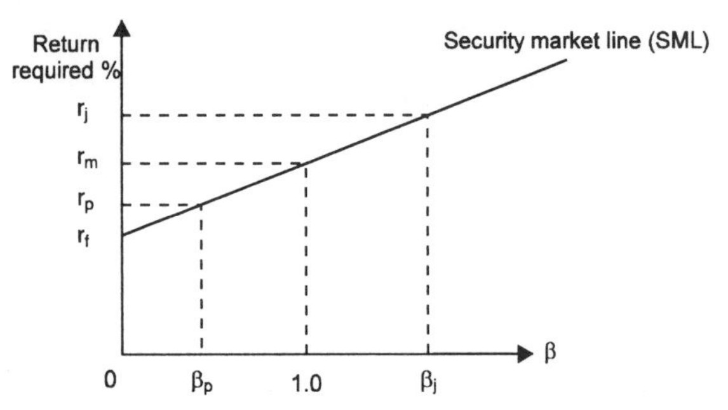

- If the investment is risk-free and $\beta = 0$, the required return will be the risk-free rate r_f
- If the investment has the same risk as the market as a whole, and $\beta = 1$, the required return will be the expected market return $E(r_m)$

For an investment with a beta of β_j, the expected return can be stated as $E(r_j)$, given by the CAPM formula:

$$E(r_j) = r_f + [E(r_m) - r_f]\,\beta_j$$

Formula given in Tables

Similarly, for a portfolio with a beta of β_p, the required portfolio return $E(r_p)$ can be stated as $r_f + [E(r_m) - r_f]\beta_p$.

Exam focus. Don't be put off balance by the fact that the Tables provided in the exam also include another version of the CAPM formula above using different notation:

$$r - r_f = \beta(r_m - r_f)$$

An *alpha factor* measures the amount by which returns on a share are greater or less than the returns that the systematic risk of a company would lead us to expect. It thus measures how wrong the CAPM is!

$\therefore E(r_j) = r_f + [E(r_m) - r_f]\,\beta_j \pm \text{alpha}$

If CAPM holds, alpha is zero.

The CAPM can be used to estimate the required return on a security, from a portfolio or from a project, for an investor expecting to get rid of unsystematic risk through diversification, and who therefore wishes to assess his required return for a given amount of non-diversifiable, systematic risk.

The CAPM produces a discount rate based on the systematic risk of the individual investment. It can therefore be used validly to compare projects of different risk classes.

The CAPM has the following limitations.

- It assumes all investors hold well diversified portfolios (ie it does not consider unsystematic risk)
- It makes the following perfect capital market assumptions
  - Investors able to invest/borrow at the same rate of interest
  - No tax
  - No transaction costs
  - Perfect information
  - Rational, risk-averse investors

- It is a single period model
- It is based on estimates which are difficult to make in practice
  - Risk-free return
  - Market return
  - β factor

In the *international case,* currency risk and market imperfections make the CAPM more difficult to apply.

Geared and ungeared betas

There is a connection between Modigliani and Miller's theories of gearing and CAPM theory, and it is possible to establish a mathematical relationship between the β value of an ungeared company and the β value of a *similar*, but geared, company.

('Similar' means a company in the same industry with the same operating and business risk characteristics, differing only in their financial gearing.)

The β value of a geared company will be higher than the β value of a company identical in every respect except that it is all-equity financed. This is because of the extra financial risk.

- Ungeared company $\rightarrow$ business risk
- Geared company $\rightarrow$ business and financial risk

An *asset beta* (β_a) measures purely business risk. The asset beta is not influenced by the method of financing.

- An ungeared company's equity beta (β_u) = asset beta (β_a)
- A geared company's equity beta (β_g) > asset beta (β_a)

Debt is generally assumed to be risk-free and its beta is then taken as zero.

The mathematical relationship between the 'ungeared' and 'geared' betas can be expressed as:

$$\beta_g = \beta_u \left[1 + \frac{D(1 - T_C)}{E} \right]$$

where β_g is the beta factor of a geared company - ie the 'geared beta'

β_u is the beta factor of a similar, but ungeared company - ie the 'ungeared beta'

D is the market value of the debt capital in the geared company

E is the market value of the equity capital in the geared company

T_C is the corporate tax rate

In the summary diagram on the next page note that:

- *Equity β* is the published β, and measures business and financial risk
- *Asset β* is the equity β, ungeared where necessary to obtain a beta free from financial risk, and measures business risk
- *Project β* is the asset β as used for project appraisal, and measures business risk of a specific project

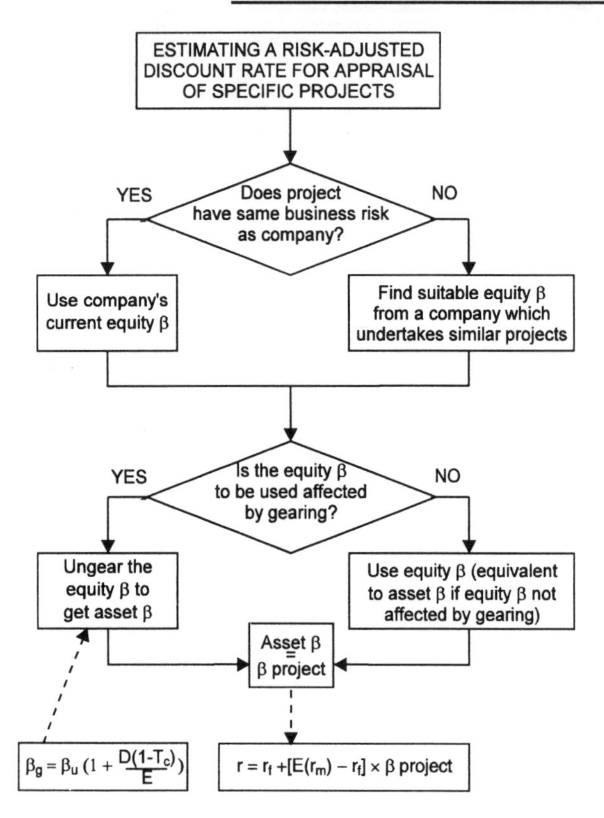
ESTIMATING A RISK-ADJUSTED DISCOUNT RATE FOR APPRAISAL OF SPECIFIC PROJECTS
Does project have same business risk as company?
YES
NO
Use company's current equity β
Find suitable equity β from a company which undertakes similar projects
Is the equity β to be used affected by gearing?
YES
NO
Ungear the equity β to get asset β
Use equity β (equivalent to asset β if equity β not affected by gearing)
Asset β = β project
$\beta_g = \beta_u (1 + \frac{D(1-T_c)}{E})$
$r = r_f + [E(r_m) - r_f] \times \beta$ project

The arbitrage pricing model

The *arbitrage pricing model* (APM) postulates that the expected return on a share depends on several independent factors, the most important of which are as follows.

- Changes in inflation
- Changes in the expected level of industrial production
- Changes in the risk premium on bonds
- Changes in the term structure of interest rates

The sensitivity of returns on a particular share to each factor will vary.

> *Exam focus.* Although *detailed* knowledge of the APM and calculations based on it will not be required, you should be prepared to discuss it as a possible alternative to the CAPM.

> *Exam focus.* SFM candidates often put too much emphasis on M&M and CAPM. Don't assume that these two topics must somehow be relevant to questions set: indeed, they did not feature at all in the 11/95 paper.

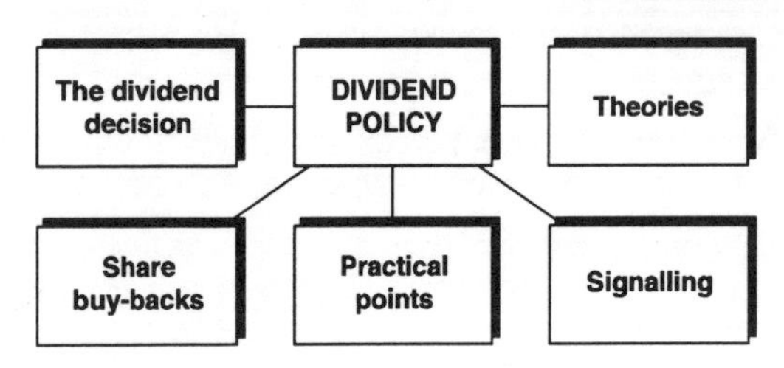

The dividend decision

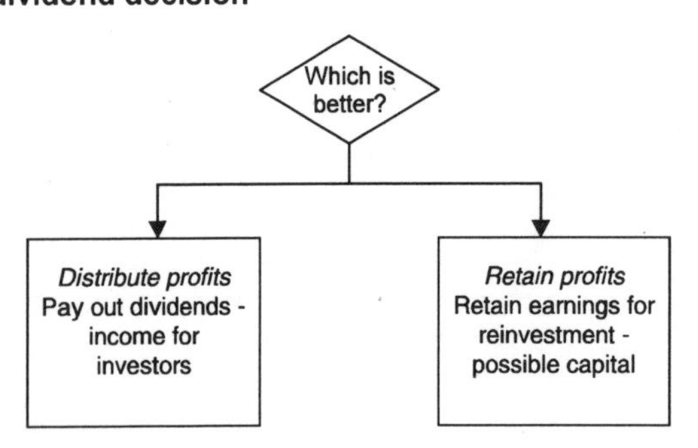

Dividend policy

5/97, 11/98

UK company dividends are subject to ACT (advance corporation tax), an up-front payment of the company's corporation tax which will eventually be set against its tax liability.

A company's directors will have a policy for:

- What proportion of profits to pay out as dividends and what proportion of profits to retain for reinvestment
- What rate of dividend growth to aim for, with the help of reinvesting retained profits

Their choice of policy might affect their company's share price.

- A high dividend payout gives shareholders more current income (on which individual shareholders pay income tax)
- A high retentions ratio should provide for future earnings and dividend growth, which ought to improve the current share price and so give investors a capital gain (on which capital gains tax would be payable if an individual investor chose to sell the shares)

A company might even *borrow* to pay dividends, provided that there is a balance of distributable profits.

It could be argued that *either* a high dividend payout ratio *or* a low dividend payout ratio, could improve share prices, depending to a large extent on the preferences of shareholders.

By a *clientele effect,* companies may attract particular types of shareholder seeking particular dividend policies.

Theories

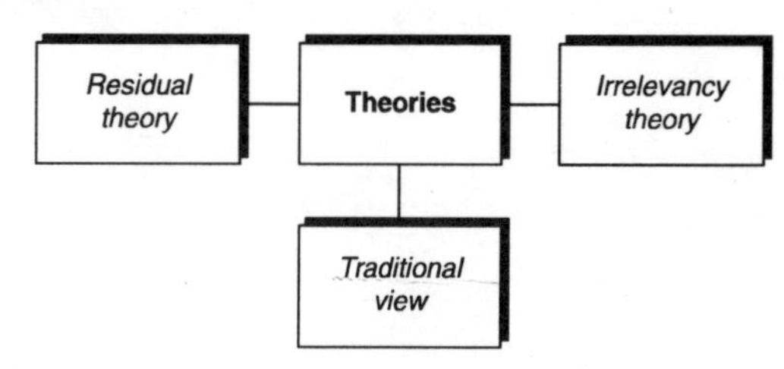

Residual theory

The residual theory can be summarised as follows.

- If a company can identify projects with positive NPVs, it should invest in them

- Only when these investment opportunities are exhausted should dividends be paid

Irrelevancy theory

An argument was put forward by Modigliani and Miller that the dividend policy of a company is *irrelevant* to its share price.

M&M argued that in a perfect and efficient capital market with no taxes, the following would apply.

- If a company pays a high dividend, it can replace the money it has paid out with an issue of new shares
  - There will be some loss of capital value to existing shareholders, but this will be exactly equal to the amount of dividend they receive
  - By making dividends higher, there will simply be an offsetting capital loss for existing shareholders, and so the new position of shareholders is the same, whatever the dividend payment ratio (0% to 100%)

- If no dividends are paid one year because of investment opportunities, shareholders can create their own income by:
  - Selling some shares, or
  - Borrowing against security of shareholding

  Shareholders can thus 'manufacture' dividends.

M&M's arguments can be criticised on the following grounds.

- Markets are not perfect in reality

- Differences in the rate of tax between dividends and capital gains will give shareholders a preference for one or the other

However, when the rates of tax on dividends and capital gains are the same, M&M's 'irrelevancy' argument about dividend policy and share prices becomes much more potent.

Traditional view

Dividends do matter! Share price depends upon the mix of dividends and growth.

$$r = \frac{d_1}{p_0} + g \quad \therefore \quad p_0 = \frac{d_1}{(r-g)} = \frac{d_0(1+g)}{(r-g)}$$

Signalling

You should appreciate the signalling aspect of dividends.

Although the market would like to value shares on the basis of underlying cash flows of the company's projects, such information is not readily available to investors. However, the directors do have this information.

- The dividend declared can be interpreted as a 'signal' from directors to shareholders about the strength of underlying project cash flows
- Directors can signal to the market in other ways also: the issue of debt, which commits the company to paying interest, can be interpreted as a signal of strong project cash flows, as compared with the issue of equity

Such 'signals' are likely to be taken as more reliable than anything which the directors say, since they involve actual commitments or movements of cash.

Practical points

5/95

Practical points relating to dividend policy are as follows.

- Issues relevant to the investor
  - o Risk - a current dividend is more certain than a future gain
  - o Taxation - some shareholders prefer dividends (eg tax-exempt pension funds); others will prefer capital gains (eg individuals who have not used their CGT allowance)
  - o Transaction costs tend to inhibit 'manufacture' of dividends
  - o Inflation

- Availability of cash
  - o The company's need to retain sufficient funds for reinvestment/ expansion
  - o Access to capital markets
  - o Repayment of debt
  - o Company taxation
  - o The company's need for surplus cash to pay a dividend

> *Exam focus.* In the 5/95 paper, a question asked if a company should borrow to pay a dividend. It might do this, provided profits are available.

- Availability of profits
  - o Legal restrictions on distributable profits
  - o Stability of profit, and therefore dividend payout
  - o Company taxation and ACT

- Dividends and share prices
  - o Management attitudes to dividend policy
  - o Dividend policy of competitors
  - o Profitability of current investment opportunities

Share buy-backs

5/97

A company with surplus cash could repurchase some of its own shares, subject to shareholders' approval.

Benefits

- Increase in EPS
- Enables increase in gearing
- Can be a way of changing equity base
- Might prevent a takeover

Disadvantages

- Setting a fair price may be a problem
- Directors may not want to admit they have no better use for funds
- Some shareholders may prefer dividends for tax reasons

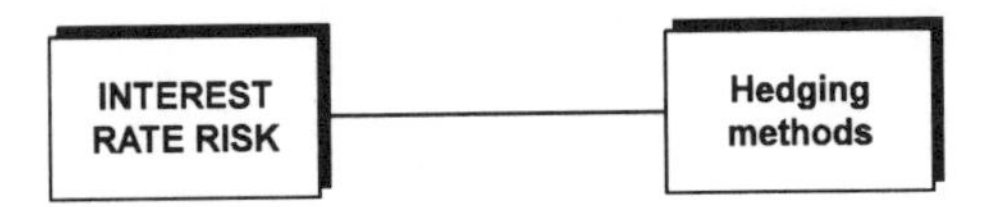

Interest rate risk

11/98

> *Exam focus.* In the 11/98 exam, an 8-mark question simply asked how interest rate risk might be managed.

There are a number of situations in which a company might be exposed to interest rate risk.

Fixed rate versus floating rate debt. A company can get caught paying higher interest rates by having fixed rather than floating rate debt, or floating rather than fixed rate debt, as market interest rates change.

Currency of debt. This is also a foreign currency exposure. A company can face higher costs if it borrows in a currency for which exchange rates move adversely against the company's domestic currency. The treasurer should seek to match the currency of the loan with the currency of underlying operations/assets that generate revenue to pay interest/repay the loans.

Term of loan. A company can be exposed by having to repay a loan earlier than it can afford to, resulting in a need to re-borrow, perhaps at a higher rate of interest.

Term loan or overdraft facility? A company might prefer to pay for borrowings only when it needs the money (overdraft facility): the bank will charge a commitment fee for a facility. Alternatively, a term loan might be preferred, but this will cost interest even if it is not needed for the whole term.

Exam focus. Where the magnitude of the risk is immaterial in comparison with the company's overall cash flows, one option you should bear in mind as you do questions on this area is to do nothing and to accept the effects of any movement in interest rates which occur.

Hedging methods

11/96

A number of treasury instruments have been devised to help a corporate treasurer to hedge exposure to material interest rate risk exposures.

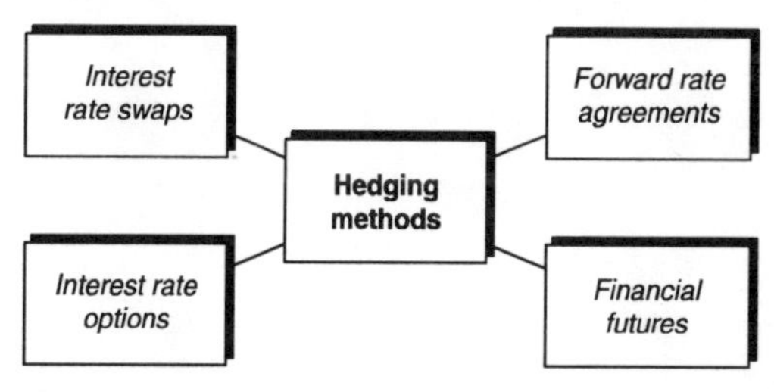

Interest rate swaps

An *interest rate swap* is an arrangement whereby two unrelated parties (Company A and Company B in the diagram below) each borrow an amount over the same term, independently of each other, one at a fixed rate and the other at a floating rate of interest. They then swap the interest payments.

Swaps can be used by a company to switch from floating rate to fixed rate borrowing, or *vice versa*.

Examples: interest rate swaps

In this example, Company A can use a swap to change from paying interest at a floating rate of LIBOR + 1% to one of paying fixed interest of ($8\frac{1}{2}$% + 1%) = $9\frac{1}{2}$%.

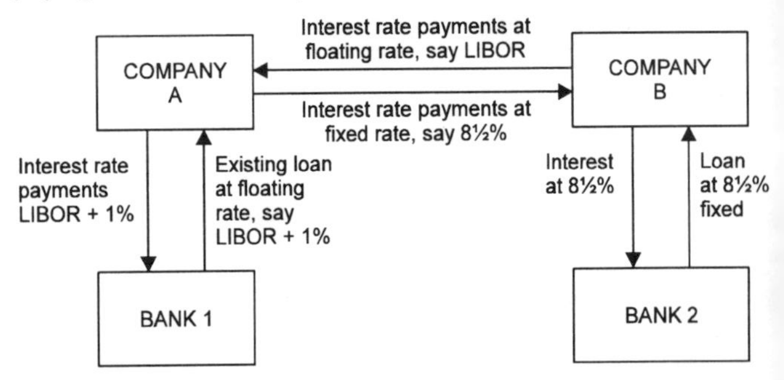

A swap counterparty will typically be found through a financial intermediary (eg a bank).

Interest rate swaps might be arranged in different currencies, for example, between a fixed rate in US dollars and a floating rate in sterling.

Where this happens, the swaps are normally reversed with the principal eventually swapped back at the original exchange rate.

For example, a UK company and a US company can arrange a back-to-back loan and currency swap as follows.

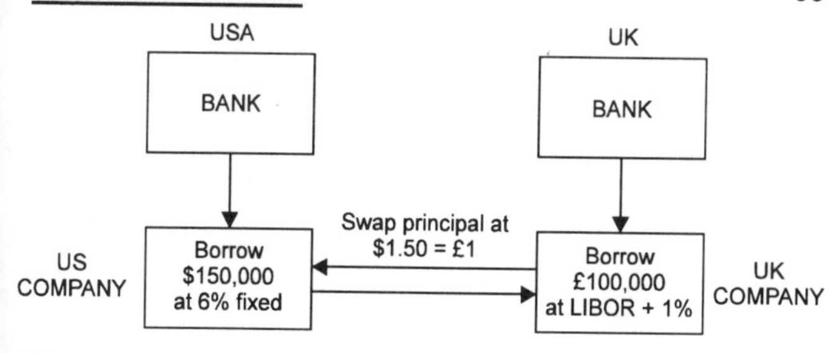

The companies can service each other's debt (interest rate swap) and also exchange the principal, with the UK company taking $150,000 and the US company taking £100,000 (currency swap). Each company will eventually repay the principal on each other's loans at a rate of $1.50 = £1.

Forward rate agreements (FRAs)

An *FRA* is an agreement between a company and a bank which fixes the interest rate in advance for a specific sum of money, which the company will invest or borrow at a specified future date.

An FRA is simply an agreement about the interest rate: it does not involve movement of the principal sum. It is usually only available on transactions above £500,000.

Financial futures

A futures contract in general is an agreement to buy or sell a standard quantity of a particular financial instrument at a specified future date at an agreed price - the price being determined by trading on the floor of a futures exchange.

For example, a company can contract to buy (or sell) £100,000 of a notional 30-year Treasury bond bearing an 8% coupon, in say, 6 months time, at an agreed price.

- The futures price is likely to vary with changes in interest rates, and this acts as a hedge against adverse interest rate movements
- The outlay to buy futures is much less than for buying the financial instrument itself, and so a company can hedge large exposures using relatively little cash

Interest rate options

Interest rate options grant the buyer the right but not the obligation to deal at an agreed interest rate (strike rate) at a future maturity date. Such options can be comparatively expensive to buy.

The term *interest rate guarantee* (IRG) is used for an interest rate option which hedges the interest rate for a single period of up to one year.

An interest rate cap is an option which sets an interest rate ceiling. Conversely, a floor sets a lower limit to interest rates.

With a *collar*, an interest rate cap is bought and an interest rate floor is sold - cheaper than obtaining a cap alone.

A *swaption* is an option to buy an interest rate swap.

Options on interest rate futures contracts are also available through LIFFE.

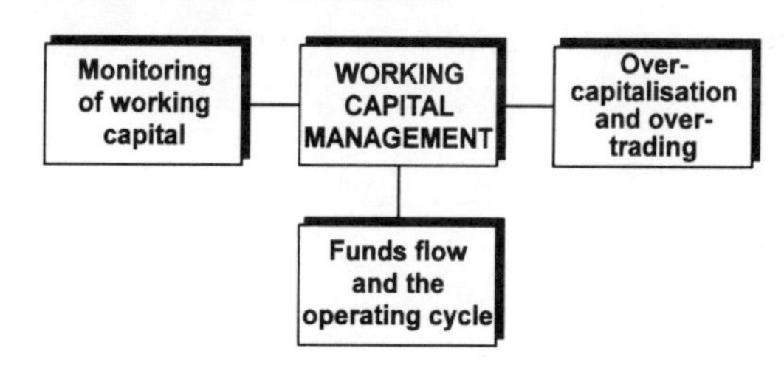

Working capital management

11/95

Working capital management involves weighing up benefits and costs of holding items of working capital to find the *optimum* policy.

Overall working capital requirements differ from business to business.

Two aspects to consider are:

- What levels of current assets to hold
- How to finance these current assets

There are various reasons for holding current assets.

- *Raw materials:* protection against price increases; avoidance of stock-outs; bulk buying advantages; flexibility for production scheduling
- *Work in progress:* may be necessary due to nature of process; policy determined by most cost-effective production methods
- *Finished goods:* sales and marketing advantages; result of production plan
- *Debtors:* sales and marketing advantages

- *Cash:* liquidity

Current assets could be financed out of:

- Current liabilities
- Long-term liabilities

Relative costs and risks need to be considered.

- *Cost:* current liabilities generally cheaper
- *Risk:* short-term credit (eg trade creditors/overdraft) could be called in

Monitoring of working capital

'Warning signs' can be given by short-term financial ratios, in particular the following.

- Sales/working capital
- Liquidity ratios:
  - Current ratio $= \dfrac{\text{Current assets}}{\text{Current liabilities}}$
  - Acid test (liquid, quick ratio) $= \dfrac{\text{Current assets - stock}}{\text{Current liabilities}}$
- Turnover periods:
  - Stock turnover period $= \dfrac{\text{Average stock}}{\text{Cost of sales}} \times 365 \text{ days}$
  - Debtors turnover period $= \dfrac{\text{Average debtors}}{\text{Sales}} \times 365 \text{ days}$
  - Creditors turnover period $= \dfrac{\text{Average creditors}}{\text{Purchases *}} \times 365 \text{ days}$

*Cost of sales if purchases figure not available

Average here means the average balance over the year.

> *Exam focus.* You should be fully fluent in calculating working capital ratios for the exam.

Over-capitalisation and overtrading

If working capital is not monitored effectively, over-capitalisation or overtrading could result.

Over-capitalisation is due to over-investment in current assets (ie working capital is excessive). The return on capital is then lower than it should be, and long-term funds are unnecessarily tied up.

Overtrading occurs when a business tries to do too much too quickly with too little long-term capital. The business could then easily run into liquidity problems if it does not have enough cash to pay debts as they fall due.

Overtrading could have the following causes.

- A business grows quickly without a corresponding growth in its capital resources
- A business repays a long-term loan without replacing it, leaving less long-term capital to finance its current level of operations

The following are symptoms of possible overtrading.

- Falls in liquidity ratios
- Rapid rise in turnover
- Rise in sales/fixed assets ratio

- Rise in stocks relative to turnover
- Increase in debtors
- Increased trade credit period
- Increased short-term borrowing/reduced cash balances
- Increase in gearing
- Fall in profit margin

Ultimately, the survival of the enterprise depends upon the maintenance of adequate working capital.

Funds flow and the operating cycle

We can think of working capital as principally stocks, debtors and short-term creditors, with cash balances and bank overdrafts as a separate item.

- An increase in working capital ties up funds, and this has consequences for cash flows
- Similarly, a reduction in working capital should speed up the inflow of cash by releasing funds

The link between working capital (stocks, debtors and creditors) and cash can be seen in the operating cycle.

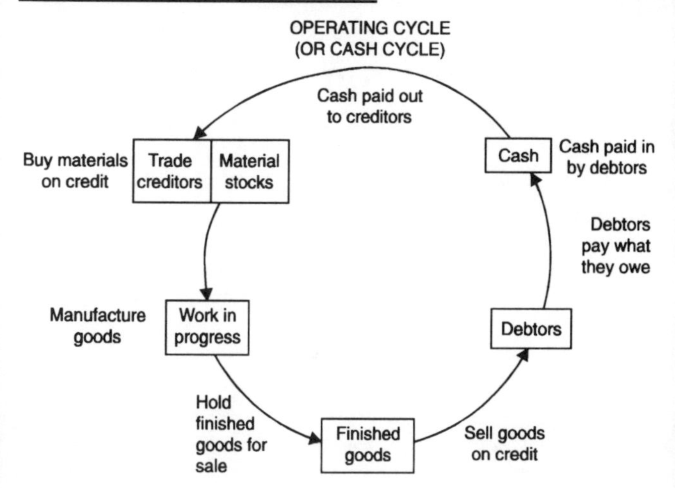

Cash flows can be improved by:

- Shorter stock turnover periods
- Shorter production cycle
- Shorter period of credit for debtors
- Longer credit taken from creditors

> *Exam focus.* An overview of the operating cycle has been provided above. We now move on to specific working capital management techniques which may come into an exam question.

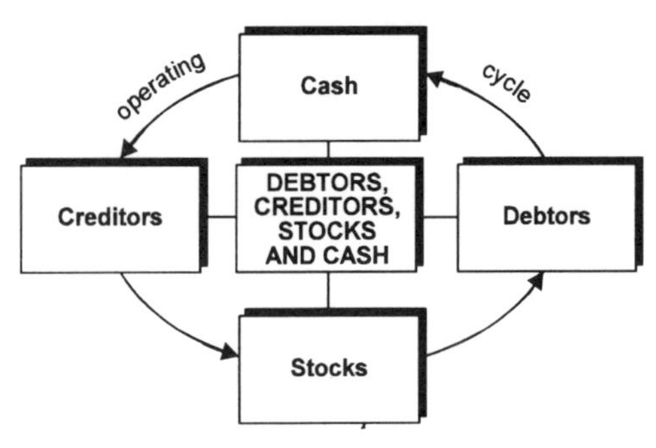

In this chapter, we cover the specifics of managing *debtors, creditors, stocks* and *cash*.

> *Exam focus.* You should be prepared for numerical questions on working capital management (eg on the cost of credit or stockholding) as well as questions requiring discussion of policy issues.
>
> You might, as in the 11/96 exam, be required to apply expected values and probabilities to a working capital problem.

Debtors 11/96, 11/97

Businesses of most types need to allow credit to achieve satisfactory sales. Allowing credit, however, results in:

- An interest cost of funds tied up in debtors (rather than immediate cash receipts)
- Possibly a bad debt risk

A balance might have to be found between sales volume, credit allowed, interest costs and bad debts.

The *credit control* function needs to assess the creditworthiness of new customers and set credit limits, using information such as the following.

- References (usually two: one from a bank)
- Credit ratings, from a credit reference agency
- Annual report and accounts of the customer company
- Extel cards
- Information gleaned from visit to the customer
- Articles from trade journals/newspapers
- DTI advice, on overseas companies

Creditworthiness of existing customers should be monitored, looking out for warning signs such as late payment or changing fortunes of the customer.

Opportunity cost of debtors = Average debtors × cost of capital

Bad debts are an additional cost.

Discounts for early payment might be used to shorten average credit periods, reduce the investment in debtors and so reduce interest costs. The benefit in interest costs saved should exceed the cost of discounts allowed.

> *Exam focus.* Questions on discounts allowed generally concern changes from the existing policy, and you then need to consider:
>
> - PV of cash inflows under current policy
> - PV of cash inflows under proposed policy

Some companies use *factoring* organisations to deal with the management of debtors.

Factors provide one or more of the following services:

- Administration of debtors - sending out invoices, sales ledger work, collecting payments
- Insurance against bad debts
- Advances against debtors, a service also provided under the name of *invoice discounting*

Advantages of factoring are as follows.

- Can reduce administration/collection costs
- Helps short-term liquidity
- Does not usually reduce borrowing capacity

Disadvantages are as follows.

- Costs
- Possible loss of customer goodwill
- Poor image

Credit insurance - insurance against bad debts - can be especially important.

With overseas debtors, there may be exchange rate risk (risk of a fall in value of debtors as exchange rates fluctuate) as well as credit risk.

Creditors

11/98

The management of *trade creditors* involves:

- Seeking satisfactory credit from suppliers
- Seeking credit extension during periods of cash shortage
- Maintaining good relations with suppliers

As debtors, on the other side of the debtor-creditor relationship from our trade creditors, suppliers will want to be sure of our creditworthiness.

In deciding whether to accept discounts offered, the problem is like a 'mirror image' of the question of allowing discounts to our customers.

Apart from trade creditors, an important source of short-term finance, the following are alternative forms of finance.

- Bank overdraft
  - Useful as temporary source of funds
  - Flexible
  - Technically repayable on demand
  - Relatively expensive
  - Variable interest rate
- Bank loan
  - Cheaper than an overdraft
  - Generally medium to longer term finance
- Secured/unsecured loan stock (debentures)
  - Secured loan stock is generally cheaper than unsecured
  - Only feasible for larger amounts required for a longer term

Stocks

Costs of holding stocks divide into four types.

- *Holding costs*, including cost of capital tied up, warehousing, deterioration, insurance and pilferage
- *Procuring costs*, or *ordering costs*

- *Shortage costs* relating to stock-outs
- *Cost of the stock itself*

A buffer stock would be held to provide for:

- Fluctuations in demand, and
- Variable supply lead times/production order cycles

A 'traditional' text book method of controlling the volume of stocks and the stock turnover period is to purchase or produce items for stock in an *'economic order quantity'* (EOQ) or batch size.

The EOQ is $\sqrt{\dfrac{2C_0D}{C_h}}$

where C_0 is the incremental cost of placing an order (or incremental set-up costs)
D is the quantity demanded per period
C_h is the holding cost per unit of stock per period

Assumptions of the EOQ formula are as follows.

- Demand is constant
- Lead time is constant
- Purchase costs are constant (no discounts)

Annual stock costs = Ordering costs + holding costs

Ordering costs = $C_0 \times$ annual number of orders = $\dfrac{C_0D}{EOQ}$

Exam focus. Although derivation of the EOQ formula is unlikely to be asked for in Paper 13, it is useful to have knowledge of the components of the formula.

Management in some manufacturing companies now aims for 'stockless production' and *Just In Time (JIT)* deliveries, whereby:

- Materials and parts are delivered from suppliers only just when they are needed
- Products are manufactured only just when they are needed for sale to customers

JIT aims towards an 'ideal' level of zero stocks, but with no hold-ups due to stock shortages.

The costs of failure of a JIT system are high, because production will be held up. So it may work best along with a *total quality management (TQM)* approach, based on the principle that the cost of preventing mistakes is less than the cost of correcting them once they occur plus the cost of lost potential for future sales.

Cash 5/96, 5/97, 11/98

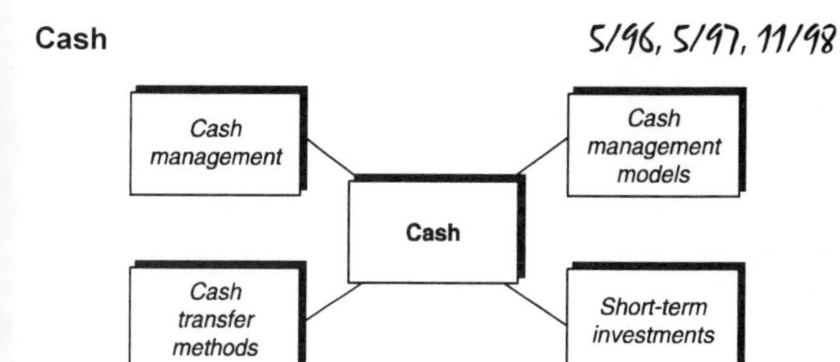

Benefits of holding cash are as follows.

- Day-to-day requirements
- Provision for unforeseen requirements

- Ability to take advantage of unforeseen business opportunities
- Ability to take advantage of cash discounts and special offers

Cash management

The *cost* of holding cash is the opportunity cost of lost interest on cash invested.

Control of cash holdings is facilitated by *cash budgets* (day-by-day, week-by-week or month-by-month forecasts of receipts and payments).

- When a company has surplus cash, this can be invested, even in the short term, to earn interest
- The treasurer should try to fund any cash deficit (overdraft) at the lowest possible cost

In large multinational companies, the planning, monitoring and control of cash will involve a number of banks and bank accounts, multi-currency facilities and computerised monitoring of cash balances.

Cash flow forecasts are also prepared for longer periods. Accurate forecasting can enable a corporate treasurer to exploit different yields from financial assets of different maturities to fund the company's cash requirements as cheaply/profitably as possible.

When a company is faced with a cash deficit in excess of its existing borrowing facilities, the treasurer can try to overcome the problem in a number of different ways, as follows.

- Increase the size of borrowing facilities
- Cancel or postpone fixed asset expenditures

- Suggest a reduction in any dividend that might be due to be announced
- Delay payments to creditors
- Make efforts to speed up payments from debtors
- Urge efforts to stimulate sales, especially cash sales
- Sell investments
- Sell any other non-essential fixed assets

Cash management models

The equation for Baumol's *inventory approach to cash management* is similar in form to the EOQ formula.

Optimum amount of securities sold =

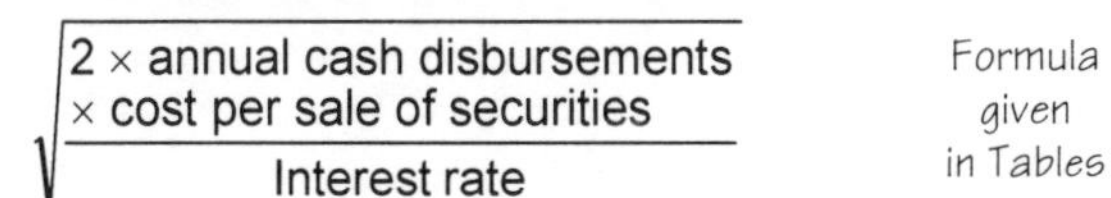

$$\sqrt{\frac{2 \times \text{annual cash disbursements} \times \text{cost per sale of securities}}{\text{Interest rate}}}$$

Drawbacks of the inventory approach are as follows.

- In practice, amounts required over future periods may not be predictable with much certainty
- There may be costs associated with running out of cash
- Other costs of holding cash may increase with the average amount held

Using the *Miller-Orr model* for cash management, the cash balance is allowed to deviate between upper and lower limits, at which points the firm buys or sells securities respectively, to bring the cash balance back to a return point at one-third of the distance (spread) between the lower and upper limits.

To apply the model, a lower limit is chosen and then the spread between upper and lower limits is computed as:

$$\text{Spread} = 3\left(\frac{3}{4} \times \frac{\text{transaction cost} \times \text{variance of cash flows}}{\text{interest rate}}\right)^{\frac{1}{3}}$$

Formula given in Tables

Not given in the CIMA *Mathematical Tables* is:

Return point = Lower limit + $^1/_3$ of spread

Once the model is established, it is easy to implement, thus saving management time. However, in practice, month-by-month cash inflows and outflows are unlikely to be entirely unpredictable as the model assumes, for example because of seasonal factors.

For any company, some large one-off payments such as dividend and tax payments will also be known well in advance, allowing for more pro-active cash management than the Miller-Orr model provides.

> *Exam focus.* A question could ask you to discuss the advantages and disadvantages of cash management models. If you are asked to apply them, any formulae required will be provided to you.

Short-term investments

Short-term investment opportunities available to the treasurer of an international company include the following.

- Money market deposits, arranged through a bank
- Local authority deposits
- Finance house deposits
- Certificates of deposit (CDs)
- Treasury bills

- Bank bills (or sterling bankers' acceptances)
- Trade bills
- Eurocommercial paper
- Eurocurrency deposits
- Eurocurrency CDs

Cash transfer methods

Electronic funds transfer saves costs and transfers funds quickly. Disadvantages are that payments must normally be made in batches, and that the speed of transfer of payments bears an interest cost compared with the slower method of paying by cheque.

There are various methods for a company to make international cash transfers, for example as follows.

- Cheque. Postal and banking clearance delays can occur. 'Lock box' bank accounts in the importer's country can be used to clear cheques speedily and then transfer funds electronically
- Bills of exchange
- Banker's draft (cheque drawn on bank)
- Mail transfers - when a bank makes a payment order to another bank overseas
- Telegraphic transfers - like a mail transfer but instructions are sent by cable or fax
- SWIFT (Society for Worldwide Interbank Financial Telecommunications). Payment messages are sent using the computer system of the member banks linked by telecommunication links
- International money orders - for small sums of money

With *multilateral netting,* debts of group companies to each other in different currencies are netted off, thus reducing transaction costs.

- First, convert the balances to the netted into a common currency
- Then, draw up a table like that below to work out the net receipt/payment for each subsidiary (figures are, say, $'000)

Receiving subsidiary	*Paying subsidiary* A	B	C	*Total*
A	-	25	50	75
B	40	-	5	45
C	70	10	-	80
Total payments	(110)	(35)	(55)	200
Total receipts	75	45	80	
Net receipt/(payt)	(35)	10	25	

To settle all the debts, A should pay $10,000 to B and $25,000 to C.

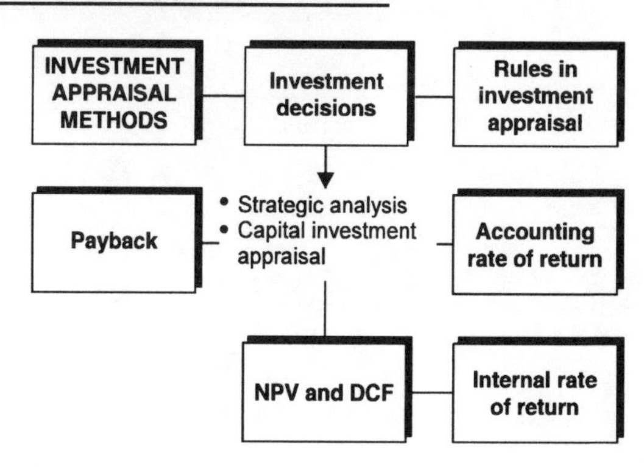

Investment decisions

5/97

Investment is any expenditure in the expectation of future benefits.

The process of investment decision making has four stages, the first two concerned with strategic analysis and the next two with capital investment appraisal.

- Strategic analysis
  - Perception of the need for investment, or awareness of a potential opportunity
  - Formulation of alternative courses of action
- Capital investment appraisal
  - Evaluation of alternative courses of action (eg using payback, ARR, DCF, NPV, IRR)
  - Choice of one alternative for implementation

Post-completion audit: a review of a project's cash flows after they have occurred, to help improve the general process of project control and appraisal.

Payback

The payback period is the time it takes for cash inflows from a capital investment project to equal the cash outflows.

The usual decision rule is either to select from competing projects the project with the shortest payback period, or to select those projects with a payback period below the organisation's target payback period.

The payback method is widely used in practice, for the following reasons.

- It is quick and simple to calculate
- The concept is easily understood by all levels of management
- Some account is taken of risk, as long payback means capital tied up for longer and thus high investment risk
- Cash flows and therefore liquidity are taken into account

Disadvantages are as follows.

- Projects which have the same payback period are not distinguished
- Any target payback period is largely arbitrary
- The method may lead to excessive investment in short-term projects
- It ignores the timing of cash flows
- It ignores the time value of money

Accounting rate of return

The accounting rate of return (ARR) is sometimes called return on capital employed (ROCE) or return on investment (ROI), and can be calculated in different ways.

> *Exam focus.* Unless the question tells you otherwise, we recommend that you adopt the following definition for the ARR.
>
> $$\text{ARR} = \frac{\text{Estimated average profits}}{\text{Estimated average investment}} \times 100\%$$

The decision rule is to accept all projects whose ARR equals or exceeds the organisation's target ARR.

Advantages of the ARR method are as follows.

- It is quick and easy to calculate
- Percentage return is a familiar concept
- It looks at the entire life of the project

Disadvantages of the method are as follows.

- It is based not on cash flows but on accounting profits, which are subject to different accounting treatments
- It takes no account of the size of the investment
- It ignores the length of the project
- It ignores the time value of money

NPV and DCF 5/96, 5/98

The *net present value* (NPV) investment criterion is based on the principles that £1 today is worth more than £1 tomorrow, and that a safe £1 is more valuable than a risky £1.

The extent to which £1 today is worth more than £1 in the future depends on the distance in time to the future cash flow and the appropriate cost of capital for discounting. Future cash flows are discounted to a present value, to give them comparability.

The NPV rule for investments by public companies is that any project with a positive NPV should be undertaken (provided that capital is available) because the market value of the company and of its ordinary shares in particular should increase by the amount of the NPV.

The cost of capital to use in NPV investment appraisal is the marginal cost of the funds raised (or earnings retained) to finance the investment.

Advantages of the NPV method are as follows.

- The method accounts correctly for the time value of money
- It uses all expected cash flows relating to the project
- It takes account of the size of the investment
- It is consistent with the objective of shareholder wealth maximisation

Disadvantages are as follows.

- There is a need to estimate a cost of capital
- The NPV concept is not easily understood

Some reminders about *discounted cash flow* (DCF) techniques are set out below.

DCF analysis might be applied to the following types of decision problem.

- Decisions whether or not to undertake a project

- Choices between mutually exclusive projects
- Decisions about how frequently to replace operational assets, eg company cars

In DCF, only relevant cash flows are discounted. A relevant cash flow is a future cash flow arising as a direct consequence of the investment decision.

- A relevant cash flow can be an extra cash cost, an extra cash revenue, savings in cash costs or reductions in cash revenue
- Non-cash items, such as absorbed fixed overheads and depreciation, should be ignored

For convenience:

- Cash flows are assumed to occur at the *end* of a time period, even though they might have occurred throughout the period
- Cash flows occurring early in a time period are assumed to occur at the end of the *previous* time period

DCF formulae

- Discount factor = $\frac{1}{(1+r)^t}$

  where r is the discount rate/interest rate

  t is the time period of the cash flow

- Annuity factor = $\frac{1}{r} - \frac{1}{r(1+r)^t}$

Formula given in Tables

The annuity factor is used for equal annual cash flows for a number of years, starting at year 1.

- Perpetuity factor = $\frac{1}{r}$ Formula given in Tables

The perpetuity factor is used for equal annual cash flows for ever, starting at year 1.

- Growing perpetuity factor = $\frac{1}{r-g}$ Formula given in Tables

This is Gordon's growth model, for cash flows growing at a constant rate g for ever.

You may also find the following formulae useful.

- For *non-annual cash flows,* the period interest rate r is related to the annual interest rate R by the following formula:

  $$r = \sqrt[n]{1+R} - 1$$

  where n is the number of periods per annum.

  Eg if the annual interest rate is 18%, the monthly interest rate r = $\sqrt[12]{1.18} - 1 = 0.0139$, ie 1.39%

- *Changes in interest rate* can be reflected as in the following example

  In years 1, 2 and 3, interest rate is 10%, 12% and 14% respectively.

  $$\text{Year 3 discount factor} = \frac{1}{(1+r_1)(1+r_2)(1+r_3)}$$

  $$= \frac{1}{1.10 \times 1.12 \times 1.14} = 0.712$$

Exam focus. A layout suitable for many investment appraisal questions is set out below.

	Time						
	0	*1*	*2*	*3*	*4*	*5*	*Note*
Sale receipts		X	X	X	X		
Costs		(X)	(X)	(X)	(X)		
Sales less costs		X	X	X	X		
Taxation			(X)	(X)	(X)	(X)	(a)
Capital expenditure	(X)						
Scrap value						X	
Working capital	(X)					X	
Tax saved:							
Capital allowances	–	–	X	X	X	X	(b)
	(X)	X	X	X	X	X	
Discount factors @ cost of capital	X	X	X	X	X	X	
Present value	(X)	X	X	X	X	X	

The NPV is the sum of the present values.

Note. You will then need supporting workings for:

(a) Taxation calculation (excluding capital allowances)
(b) Capital allowances

Rules in investment appraisal

Include

- Effect of tax allowances
- After-tax incremental cash flows
- Working capital requirements
- Opportunity costs

Exclude

- Depreciation
- Dividend/interest payments (∵ dividend/borrowing decisions analysed separately)
- Sunk costs
- Allocated costs and overheads

Internal rate of return

5/97

With the NPV method, present values are calculated by discounting at a target rate of return or cost of capital. The NPV is the difference between the present value of costs and the present value of benefits.

In contrast, the internal rate of return (IRR) method is to calculate the exact DCF rate of return which the project is expected to achieve, ie the rate at which the NPV is zero.

- The first step is to calculate two NPVs, preferably one positive and one negative and both close to zero
- Interpolation is then used to find the IRR

Advantages of the IRR method are as follows.

- It usually results in the same decision as the NPV method
- The concept of percentage return is easily understood

Disadvantages are as follows.

- The method is not suitable where there are non-conventional cash flows, which may produce multiple IRRs
- The IRR could be confused with ARR, which is a different measure
- The IRR method ignores the size of the investment
- It assumes reinvestment of cash generated at the IRR of the original project, which could be an unreasonable assumption
- Mutually exclusive projects may be ranked incorrectly

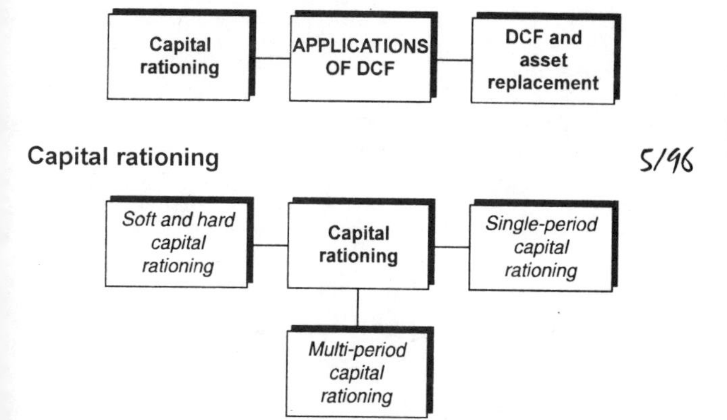

Capital rationing

> *Exam focus.* For Paper 13, it is important to understand the advantages and disadvantages of capital rationing procedures.

Soft and hard capital rationing

When capital for investments is in restricted supply, a choice must be made between projects that all have a positive NPV.

- *Soft* or internal capital rationing is where capital is rationed by constraints within the business (which might include management reluctance to raise further capital and thus dilute EPS or allow in new outside shareholders)
- *Hard* or external capital rationing is where external forces limit the amount of capital available to a business (which might include government policies on credit)

Single-period capital rationing

If capital rationing is in the current time period only:

- And projects/investments are *not divisible*, the feasible combination of projects that give the highest total NPV should be selected
- And projects/investments are *divisible*, the projects for selection should be ranked according to a *profitability index (PI)*, ie descending order of NPV of future net cash flows per £1 of current outlay, since this will give the highest achievable NPV

The PI approach has the following limitations.

- Projects are assumed to be infinitely divisible, which is unlikely to be true in practice
- Project returns are assumed to rise in proportion to the amount invested in each project
- No account is taken of the different levels of risk of different investments
- A simple PI approach cannot be used where additional funds are available at higher cost

Multi-period capital rationing

If capital rationing is in more than one time period, a *linear programming* (LP) model can be set up to establish which projects to select.

> *Exam focus.* You will not be expected to formulate a linear programming model in a Paper 13 question.

DCF and asset replacement

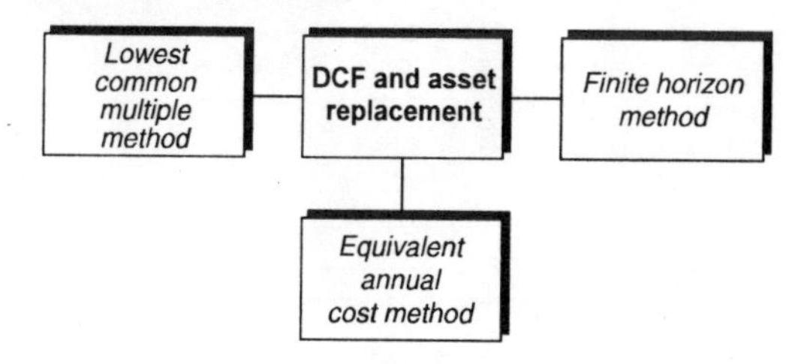

DCF techniques can be used in asset replacement decisions. Remember the three basic methods of deciding the optimum replacement cycle. Each will give the same result.

Lowest common multiple method

Estimate cash flows over a period which is the lowest common multiple of the replacement cycles and discount these over the lowest common multiple time period, to find the cycle with the lowest present value of cost.

Finite horizon method

Calculate the present value of costs over a significant period (of perhaps 15 or 20 years).

Equivalent annual cost method

Calculate the PV of cash flows over one replacement cycle and turn this into an equivalent annual cost (by dividing this PV by the cumulative PV factor for the number of years in the cycle), ie:

An asset with a life of t years has an equivalent annual cost of:

$$\frac{\text{PV costs}}{\text{t - year annuity factor}}$$

Formula given in Tables

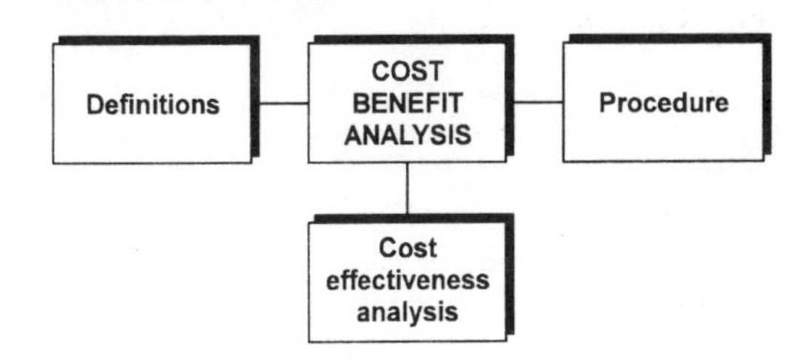

Definitions

Cost benefit analysis (CBA) is 'a comparison between the cost of the resources used, plus any other costs imposed by an activity (eg pollution, environmental damage) and the value of the financial and non-financial benefits derived' (CIMA).

The term is often used to describe investment decision-making techniques in a non profit making organisation, eg a central or local government department.

Surrogate price, a term used in CBA, refers to the price consumers would pay *if* a market existed for something.

Procedure

11/96

CBA attempts to quantify environmental and other social costs and benefits, eg by:

- Putting money values on them ('shadow prices')
- Treating them as cash flows
- Discounting along with 'economic' cash flows at an appropriate discount rate

Cost effectiveness analysis

With 'cost effectiveness analysis', costs and resources committed are measured in monetary terms but benefits in non-monetary terms.

Exam focus. The Examiner has stated that it is unlikely that cost benefit analysis will be tested in a quantitative way.

Cost of capital and investment appraisal

As well as being the cost of funds that a company uses, the *cost of capital* is the minimum return a company should be making on its investments. Using the *dividend valuation model* (DVM), we get the following result.

If a company undertakes a project, which is financed so that its cost of capital (WACC) remains unchanged, the total market value of its equity (ordinary shares) will increase by the amount of the NPV of the project (calculated using the WACC as discount rate).

If the market has strong form efficiency, the shares will increase in value as soon as details of the project become known.

The *CAPM* (see Chapter 15) can be used instead of the DVM to establish a cost of capital to use in investment appraisal.

The two models produce different values because:

- The DVM uses expectations of dividends (affected by unsystematic risk variations) and actual share values (which may not be in equilibrium)
- The CAPM considers systematic risk only, and assumes stock market equilibrium

Adjusted present value method 5/98

The adjusted present value (APV) method of project evaluation is a technique that can be used where the method of financing the project means that using the company's WACC to discount the cash flows would be inappropriate.

Instead, a 'base-case' NPV is calculated and the positive or negative effects of the selected method of financing are then added to or subtracted from the NPV to reach an APV.

A project's APV can be described as:

- A 'base case' NPV, assuming all-equity finance and a cost of capital appropriate to this
- *Plus or minus* the PV of 'side effects' of undertaking the project, such as
  - The PV of costs of raising the finance
  - The PV of the benefits of the 'tax shield', if the project is debt-financed, representing tax relief available on the *debt capacity* generated by the project, not on the amount *actually* borrowed. Tax savings are discounted at the *pre-tax* cost of capital

> *Exam focus.* If information on the debt capacity generated is not given in a question, then use the actual amount borrowed.

The APV approach suggests that it is possible to calculate an *adjusted cost of capital* (r^*), using one of three formulae below. (The opportunity cost of capital is r.)

M & M formula

Use if borrowing capacity is a constant percentage of initial project value.

$$r^* = r(1 - T^*L)$$

Formula given in Tables

where T^* is the net tax saving, expressed in pounds, of £1 of future debt interest payments (ie as a decimal)

L is the marginal contribution of the project to the debt capacity of the firm, expressed as a proportion of *the present value of the project*

Miles-Ezzell formula

Use if borrowing is kept at a constant percentage of changing project value.

$$r^* = r - Lr_D T^* \left(\frac{1+r}{1+r_D}\right)$$

Formula given in Tables

where r_D is the rate of interest on borrowings

Weighted average cost of capital (WACC) formula

All of the variables in this formula refer to the firm as a whole, and therefore the formula only works for projects with the same risk as the firm which undertakes them.

$$r^* = r_D(1 - T_c)\frac{D}{E+D} + r_E\frac{E}{E+D}$$

Formula given in Tables

where r_D is the firm's current borrowing rate

T_c is the marginal corporate tax rate

r_E is the expected rate of return on the firm's shares (which depends on the firm's business risk and its debt ratio)

D, E are the market values of currently outstanding debt and equity respectively

Exam focus. The examiner has stated that, of the three formulae shown above, the WACC formula is likely to be the choice in examinations, but that you should be aware of the other methods and understand what the terms mean. The M&M and Miles-Ezzell formulae are mainly of academic interest.

DCF and inflation

When dealing with inflation in investment appraisal, all cash flows need to be treated consistently, on either a 'real' or a nominal ('money') basis.

Real and money rates of return are linked by the following formula.

$$(1 + \text{money rate}) = (1 + \text{real rate}) \times (1 + \text{inflation rate})$$

Cash flows may be 'real' or 'money' cash flows.

- *Real cash flows* are cash flows, including future cash flows, expressed in current price terms, ie with the effect of inflation removed
- *Money cash flows* are expressed in terms of the actual amounts of money that will be received at the various future dates

'Real' and 'money' discount rates may be distinguished as follows.

- The *real discount rate* is the rate of return required if there were no inflation
- The *money discount rate* is the return required given that inflation will occur

The rules are then as follows.

- Discount *real* cash flows at a *real* discount rate
- Discount *money* cash flows at a *money* discount rate

Future inflation in prices and costs is almost inevitable.

If all prices and costs are expected to increase at the same percentage rate, inflation in cash flows can be ignored *provided that* the cash flows are discounted at a real cost of capital.

Alternatively, all prices and costs should be increased to allow for expected inflation, and the inflated cash flows discounted at the money cost of capital. Market rates of interest are a money cost of capital. This approach is especially suitable when costs and revenues are expected to rise in price at different rates.

DCF and taxation 5/98

The effects of taxation on cash flows should be included in DCF analysis, with after-tax cash flows discounted at an after-tax cost of capital.

Taxation on profits is often assumed to be at a standard percentage rate, and (typically) payable one year in arrears. As a general convention, taxation is assessed as a percentage of cash profits, but this is not a hard and fast rule.

There may be capital allowances on capital equipment purchases.

Exam focus. Capital allowances could be in the form of a writing down allowance, but you will need to check capital allowance details in any question you attempt.

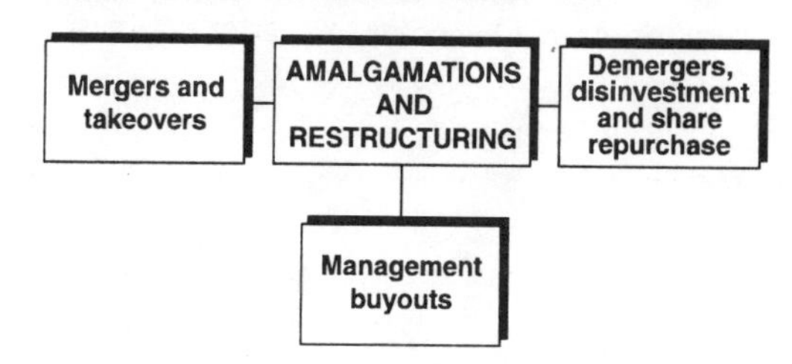

Amalgamations and restructuring 11/96

Amalgamating and restructuring may take various forms, for example:

- Mergers and takeovers
- Demergers
- Buyouts and buyins

> *Exam focus.* As in the 11/96 case study involving a family-owned company facing financial difficulties and the threat of liquidation, you may be expected to evaluate a situation from the viewpoints of owners, managers and potential investors and to formulate a new financial and operational strategy.

Mergers and takeovers 5/95, 11/97

Mergers and takeovers are essentially the same thing, except that mergers refer to the joining together of two firms of comparable size, and takeovers refer to a combination following which the management of one of the combining firms will be dominant.

Possible reasons for growth by acquisition include the following.

- Synergistic effects (2 + 2 = 5)

- Operating economies - eliminating inefficiency
- Acquisition of patents, brands or management skills
- Bolstering of asset backing
- Improving quality of earnings
- Finance/liquidity
- Reduction in risk and cost of capital
- Eliminating competition - increased power in the market
- Gaining of monopoly power
- Economies of vertical integration
- Opportunities to acquire undervalued assets

The purchase price must be decided and agreed between the directors/shareholders of the companies involved.

If the target company's shares have a market price, a successful takeover bid will need to offer a higher price, to win acceptances of the offer.

There are the following factors to consider in an amalgamation.

- Target companies may be over-valued because of
  - Over-optimism regarding economies of scale
  - The share price of the victim company already anticipating the synergistic gains
  - The victim's share price being 'bid up' in an auction
  - General uncertainties in the valuation
- Will shareholders in the predator company regard the takeover as desirable?
- Do shareholders want cash or capital gains?
- Are the owners of the target company amenable?
- How will the takeover influence the financial statements?

- Are there any other potential problems?

The predator company will wish to consider the purchase consideration, which could be:

- Cash
- Shares in the predator company in exchange for shares in the target company (a share exchange perhaps with a cash alternative)
- New loan stock in the predator company, perhaps convertible into equity at a future date

The nature of the purchase consideration (cash or 'paper offer') will affect the EPS and share values after the takeover.

If the takeover bid involves an all-share offer, and the profits of the enlarged company after the merger are no larger than the profits of the separate companies before the merger:

- There will be 'earnings concentration' for the shares that were valued on a higher P/E ratio for the purpose of the takeover
- There will be 'earnings dilution' for the shares valued on a lower P/E ratio

If the purchase consideration involves a share exchange, the target company's shareholders will also want to consider how:

- Dividends, and
- Asset backing per share

might be affected if they accept shares in the predator company.

Takeover bids might be welcomed by the directors of the target company, or viewed as hostile. In the event of a hostile bid, the target company's directors will take defensive measures to persuade their shareholders to turn down the bid, such as the following.

- Contesting the offer on: terms being poor, no obvious advantage, employee opposition
- Issuing forecasts to indicate sale of shares (not a good option)
- Revaluing assets
- Advertising (subject to City Code)
- Lobbying to have the offer referred to the MMC
- Finding a 'white knight' (an alternative, more acceptable bidder)
- Arranging a management buyout
- 'Poison pill' tactics: the target builds in a tripwire to make itself less attractive, eg creating a new class of stock which automatically becomes redeemable at a high price in the event of a takeover

In the UK, the takeover of public companies is subject to the City Code on Takeovers and Mergers mentioned above. In addition, takeovers that may be against the public interest can be referred to the Monopolies and Mergers Commission (MMC) by the Office of Fair Trading/Department of Trade and Industry. The MMC has the power to stop a takeover.

Reasons for post-acquisition failure include the following.

- Paying too high a price
- Failure to take decisive action to restructure following an acquisition

- Poor strategy
- Lack of objectivity in researching a company (possibly coloured by personal ambition)
- Synergies being over-estimated (eg Prudential's move into estate agency in the late 1980s)
- Market downturn
- Excessively high gearing
- Poor internal control
- Excessive concern over synergies while failing to focus on market growth potential

Factors leading to successful acquisitions include those below.

- Many are the opposites of the above list
- The acquiring company needs to assess what it can offer the acquired company
- The two companies should have something in common
- Key executive insurance should be taken out in case key personnel leave the acquired company
- Within a year, management should have moved between companies
- Clear control procedures need to be put in place

Merger and acquisition activity in different countries can be compared.

- The UK and US have relatively high levels of takeover activity, often hostile in nature

- The US has strong anti-trust legislation outlawing monopolies and restricting the number of horizontal amalgamations
- There has been a growth in takeover activity in Europe reflecting the growing importance of this market to the rest of the world and its growing competitiveness
- In Japan, banks play a much greater part in funding and guiding companies and there is less aggressive merger activity

> *Exam focus.* Business amalgamations (mergers and takeovers) have always been a key topic for exam questions.

Demergers, disinvestment and share repurchase 5/95

Companies do not always seek growth. Some might seek:

- To separate the different parts of their business into independent companies, and give shareholders new shares in each newly established company in a demerger (eg ICI and its former pharmaceuticals division Zeneca; British Gas)
- To sell unprofitable subsidiaries
- To repurchase some of their own shares (see Chapter 16), usually if the company has a large amount of cash for which it cannot find a worthwhile investment use (as have a number of the privatised UK electricity companies recently)

Management buyouts

A management buyout (MBO) is the purchase of all or part of a business from its owners by one or more of its executive managers.

The parties to a buyout are:

- The management team
- The directors of the company/group
- The financial backers of the management team (eg merchant banks; venture capitalists)

The following are reasons for a buyout.

- From the buyout team's point of view:
    - To obtain ownership of the business rather than remain as employees
    - To avoid redundancy if the business is threatened with closure
- From the directors' point of view:
    - To dispose of a part of the company/group that perhaps does not fit in with the overall strategy of the company/group
    - To dispose of a loss-making segment of the business which the directors do not have the time or inclination to turn around
    - To raise cash
    - To avoid having to try and sell off parts of a business in the open market
    - To avoid redundancy costs or strike action where closure is the only alternative

The following are advantages of an MBO:

- Personal motivation of the buyout team
- A more hands-on approach to management
- Keener decision making on such areas as pricing and debt collection

- Savings in head office overheads

The following are possible problems:

- Lack of experience of the management team
- Tax and legal complications
- Motivation of employees not party to the buyout
- Lack of additional finance once the buyout has taken place
- Maintenance of previous commitments made by the company to the workforce or others
- Loss of key employees
- Excessive interest payment burdens

A *management buyin* (MBI) has many of the same advantages and disadvantages as an MBO.

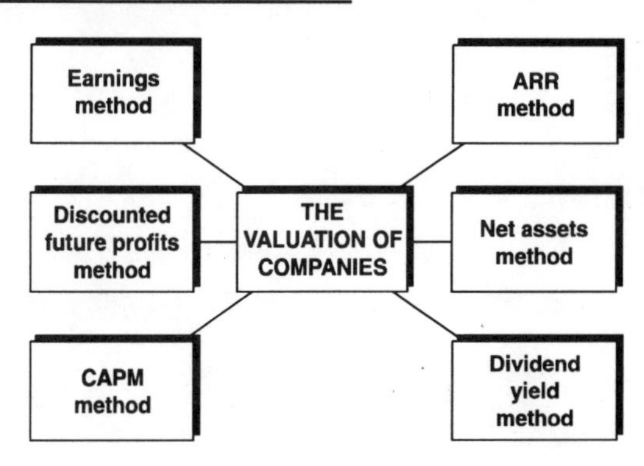

The valuation of companies 5/95, 11/96, 11/97, 5/98

Why value a business? Reasons are as follows.

- To sell a business
- To buy a business
- To float a company
- On reconstruction, merger or takeover

The major considerations are as follows.

- Size of holding
- Reactions of other shareholders
- Reasons for sale
- Liquidity

Valuation cannot be exact - an 'art' rather than a 'science'.

Earnings method

Since $\text{P/E ratio} = \dfrac{\text{Market value}}{\text{EPS}}$

Value per share = EPS × P/E ratio

This is the most common basis for valuing a going concern.

A predator company sometimes uses their (higher) P/E ratio to value a target company. This assumes that the predator can improve the target's business - a dangerous assumption. It would be better to use an adjusted industry P/E ratio, or some other method.

ARR method

$$\text{Value of a business} = \frac{\text{Estimated future profits}}{\text{Required ROCE}}$$

In a takeover bid situation, it may be necessary to adjust the profits figure to allow for expected changes after the takeover.

Net assets method

$$\text{Value per share} = \frac{\text{Value of net assets}}{\text{Number of shares}}$$

Include only those assets attributable to that class of share.

Amendments may need to be made to the balance sheet value of assets.

- Add marketable intangible assets (brands, trademarks)
- Revalue fixed assets
- Assess whether all stock is saleable

- Establish whether all debts are collectable

This basis of valuation is appropriate in an 'asset stripping' situation. It normally represents a minimum price which the selling company will accept.

Dividend yield method

For constant dividends:

$$\text{Value per share} = \frac{\text{Gross dividend per share}}{\text{Dividend yield}}$$

With dividend growth, the dividend growth model for share valuation can be used:

$$p_0 = \frac{d_1}{(r - g)}$$

The dividend yield method is suitable for valuing minority interests in unquoted companies.

CAPM method

The CAPM might be used to value shares, particularly when pricing shares for a stock market listing.

- Decide on a suitable beta factor for the company's equity (eg the beta of a company in the same industry with similar gearing)
- Calculate the cost of equity using the CAPM formula
- Use the dividend growth model to calculate the market value of the shares

Discounted future profits method

The acquisition of the target business is treated like any other project.

The maximum price to pay is one which would make the return from all cashflows involved in the investment equal to the company's cost of capital over the period, so that the NPV would be 0.

This method of share valuation may be appropriate when one company intends to buy the assets of another company and to make further investments in order to improve profits in the future.

> *Exam focus.* In the 5/95 exam, candidates were asked to choose and to apply different valuation models to a company in the event that it adopts either of two alternative dividend policies. That question included formulae which used different notation from those in the CIMA Mathematical Tables. Do not allow such differences to confuse you. You may use formulae given in the question, or in the *Tables*, or from elsewhere, provided that you make clear what the terms included mean.

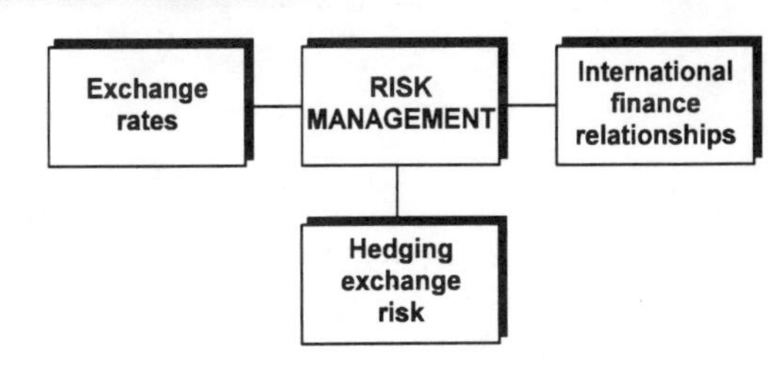

Exchange rates

11/95, 5/98

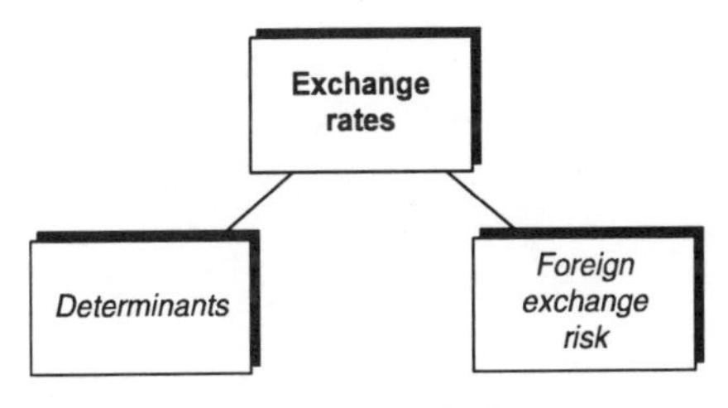

An exchange rate is the rate at which one currency can be traded in exchange for another currency.

Currencies are bought and sold on the foreign exchange (FX) markets either:

- *Spot* - for immediate delivery, or
- *Forward* - for delivery at a date in the future

Banks will quote spot rates for buying and selling currency.

For example, the US$/£ spot rate might be quoted as 1.5400 - 1.5420

The bank will sell US$ at $1.5400 to £1 and will buy US$ at $1.5420 to £1.

Of the spot rates quoted, the lower rate is always the bank's selling rate and the higher rate is always the bank's buying rate.

Forward rates are quoted by banks at a premium or discount to the spot rate. The 'ADDIS' rule applies - *add* a *dis*count to the spot rate, or subtract a premium, to obtain the forward rate.

Forward rates *do not* represent the FX markets' expectations about what exchange rates will be in the future

- The difference between spot rates and forward rates reflects interest rate differentials between the two currencies
- The principle of *interest rate parity* thus links the foreign exchange markets and the international money markets

$$\frac{1 + r_{SFr}}{1 + r_{\$}} = \frac{f_{SFr/\$}}{s_{SFr/\$}}$$

Formula given in Tables

where r_{SFr} is the Swiss franc (or other currency A) interest rate on a deposit for a certain time period

$r_{\$}$ is the dollar (or other currency B) interest rate on a deposit for the same time period

$f_{SFr/\$}$ is the forward exchange rate Sfr/$ (or A/B) for the same time period

$s_{SFr/\$}$ is the spot exchange rate SFr/$ (or A/B)

If this interest rate parity relationship did not hold, then speculators would be able to make money by arbitrage.

Purchasing power parity theory predicts that exchange rates will adjust towards levels such that when an amount of one currency is exchanged into another, the amount of the second currency has the same purchasing power as the amount of the first currency which was exchanged.

This means that exchange rates should adjust to reflect different rates of inflation in different countries, with the proportionate change in the spot exchange rate being given by the following formula.

$$\frac{i_f - i_{uk}}{1 + i_{uk}}$$

where i_f is the expected price inflation in the foreign country

i_{uk} is the expected price inflation in the domestic country

In practice, the predictions of purchasing power parity theory hold in the long run only. Short-run exchange rate movements are more likely to be due to other factors.

> *Exam focus.* The application of purchasing power parity theory is an important exam technique. Make sure that you can use the formula above.

Determinants

The exchange rate between currencies is determined by supply and demand for the currencies involved, which are in turn influenced by:

- Relative rates of inflation
- Relative rates of interest (an increase in relative interest rate should boost demand for the currency as investors switch funds into that currency)

- The levels of imports and exports (the balance of payments)
- Speculation
- Government policy or intervention to influence the exchange rate, or membership of an exchange rate system (see below)
- The sentiment of international financial markets regarding relative economic prospects of different countries

Foreign exchange risk

Foreign exchange risk exposure for companies with assets and/or liabilities denominated in foreign currencies or income/ expenditure in foreign currencies can be divided into three categories.

Translation exposure. These are potential losses that might occur when foreign currency assets or liabilities are translated into domestic currency for the preparation of the company's consolidated accounts.

Transaction exposure. Where a company is to receive or pay an amount of money in a foreign currency at some time in the future, transaction exposure arises from risk of adverse exchange rate movements between now and the eventual cash receipt/payment. Adverse movements might wipe out profits on a contract to supply goods at a pre-agreed price in a foreign currency.

Economic exposure. This arises from the effect of adverse exchange rate movements on future cash flows, where no contractual arrangement to receive or pay money has yet been made. This kind of exposure is longer term in nature and difficult to quantify exactly.

International finance relationships 5/98

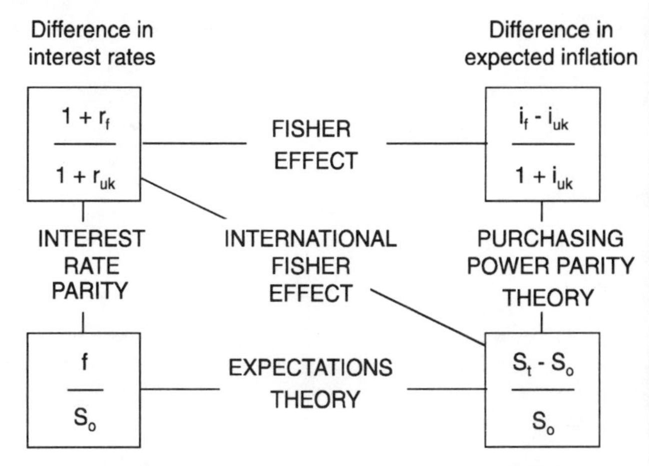

How closely does each relationship hold?

- Because of arbitrage, *interest rate parity* virtually always holds
- The *Fisher effect* suggests that *real* interest rates are the same everywhere: there is only limited evidence that this applies
- *Purchasing power parity* theory holds fairly well for *expected* changes
- *Expectations theory* assumes that traders don't care about risk, but holds on average

Hedging exchange risk

11/96, 5/97, 11/97, 5/98

Various methods are available for reducing ('hedging') foreign exchange risk.

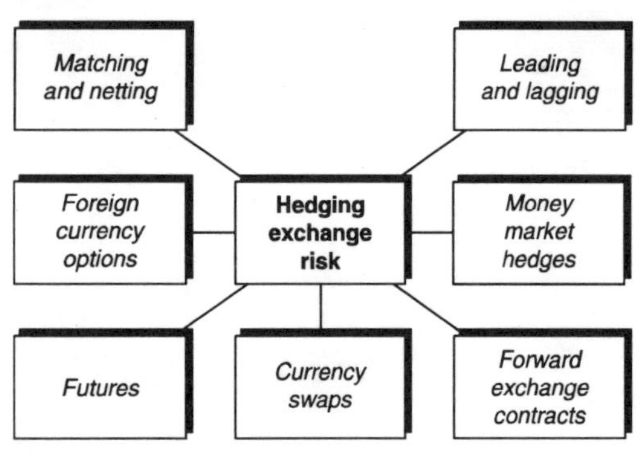

Matching and netting

Matching the currencies of fixed asset and long-term liabilities serves to reduce or eliminate translation exposure.

Netting and matching of foreign currency inflows and outflows can reduce transaction exposure. A company can try:

- To buy supplies in the same currencies in which it earns revenue
- To use the foreign currency income to pay the supplier

Leading and lagging

A company might:

- Make payments in advance (*leading*), or
- Delay payments beyond their due date (*lagging*)

Leading and lagging can be used to reduce the transaction risk of adverse exchange rate movements (hedging) or to take advantage of expected favourable exchange rate movements (speculation). Interest costs of advance payments need to be considered.

> *Exam focus.* Bear in mind that in hedging risk, it is *net* exposure which matters. For example, if a UK company expects to receive $10 million and to pay $4 million, both in three months time, the exposure to be hedged is $6 million receivable. Using the *net* figure in an exam question will gain marks.

Money market hedges

An exporter who invoices foreign customers in a foreign currency could hedge against the transaction risk by:

- Borrowing an amount in the foreign currency immediately
- Converting the foreign currency into domestic currency at the spot rate
- Repaying the loan with interest out of the eventual foreign currency receipts

This is a *money market hedge*. A company can also use a money market hedge to make a foreign currency payment in the future, buying the currency now at the spot rate and putting it on deposit, then using the principal and the interest earned to make the foreign currency payment when it falls due.

Forward exchange contracts

A forward exchange contract is:

- An immediately firm and binding contract between a bank and its customer

- For the purchase or sale of a specified quantity of a stated foreign currency
- At a rate of exchange fixed at the time the contract is made
- For performance (ie delivery of the currency and payment for it) at a future time which is agreed upon when making the contract: this future time will be either a specific date, or at any time between two specified dates

Note that in a money market hedge, currency is purchased now, while in a forward exchange contract, delivery takes place at a future date.

In deciding between the forward exchange market and the money market (or other hedging methods), the cheaper option should be chosen.

> *Exam focus.* As in the 5/98 exam, questions may expect you to be aware of how the European common currency zone, which the UK will not be joining at the outset, affects hedging requirements of businesses. The currency risk that existed between the old currencies in the zone will disappear.

Currency swaps

With a currency swap, the parties swap equivalent amounts of currency for a period. This allows a debt in one currency to be exchanged for a debt in another.

As with interest rate swaps (discussed later), there is *counterparty risk:* if the other party defaults, the original borrower remains liable to the lender.

Swaps may help in reducing transaction costs, taxation or unwanted effects on published balance sheets.

Futures

Some financial futures markets (but not LIFFE - the London International Futures and Options Exchange) offer foreign currency futures.

A foreign currency future is an agreement for the sale or purchase of a *standard* quantity of a foreign currency at a specified future time and exchange rate.

- Futures are available in only a limited number of currencies
- They are an alternative to forward exchange contracts but, being standardised in amounts and delivery dates, are less flexible

Unlike with forward exchange contracts, a currency futures position can be (and most often is) '*closed out*' by selling the futures contract in the market to realise any profit or loss without actually taking delivery of the underlying currency. (For some other types of future, eg stock index futures, delivery is not possible.)

It may help to think of a futures contract as being like a 'bet' on how exchange rates or other prices will move: however, like other derivatives, futures are of use to those who wish to hedge (reduce risk) as well as those who seek speculative risk-taking opportunities.

Futures can be used to 'lock in' exchange rates by offsetting any losses on the spot market when foreign currency is actually purchased or sold with gains on the futures market.

Futures contracts involve *margin payments* (a security deposit). Day-to-day changes in the value of the contract must also be paid for by means of the 'variation margin'.

Basis risk is a term used to describe the risk that the futures price may move differently from the spot market price.

Foreign currency options

A currency option or foreign currency option can be described as a contract by which the buyer of the option has the right, *but is not obliged*, to buy (call option) or sell (put option) a certain quantity of a currency at a specified rate of exchange (the exercise price) within a certain limited time or at the end of that time.

The absence of an obligation to buy or sell the currency is what makes it different from (and more expensive to obtain than) a forward exchange contract.

As well as protecting against risk, currency options allow companies to gain from favourable exchange rate movements.

Options (as well as other derivatives such as futures) can be combined to achieve various hedging strategies. One example is the *zero cost collar*, which can be achieved as follows.

- The company purchases a put option to sell a foreign currency at a certain exercise price
- At the same time, the company writes a put option at a lower price (ie exchange rate)

This arrangement limits the exchange rate faced by the company to within a known range. If the premium on the option written is the same as the premium on the option purchased, then the hedge has 'zero cost'.

> *Exam focus.* In an exam question, you could be required to compare costs of different hedging strategies under different outcomes.

Investments as options on future cash flows

Various business decisions can be analysed in terms of the *options* they involve, such as the option to:

- make follow-on investments (equivalent to a call option)
- abandon a project (equivalent to a put option)
- wait before making an investment (equivalent to a call option)

Unlike with traded options, there is no market for such options, and so valuing them is a subjective exercise.

> *Exam focus.* The topic of investments as options on future cash flows is new to the syllabus for May 1998: so be prepared for it to be examined fairly early in the life of the new syllabus.

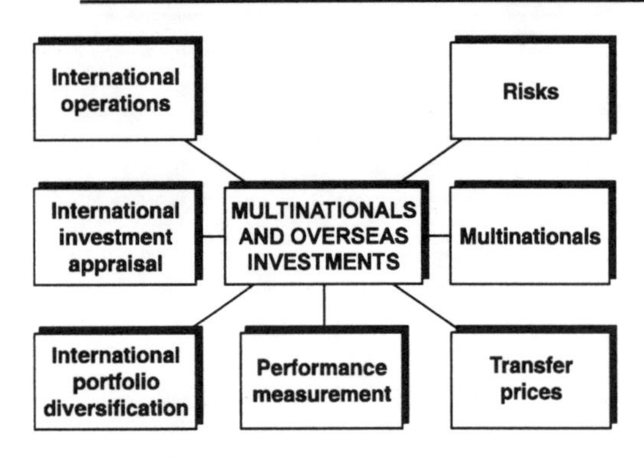

International operations 11/95, 5/97, 11/98

While international trade brings advantages, exporting can have the following drawbacks.

- High transport costs to foreign markets
- Tariffs, quotas and regulations
- Preference of consumers for locally produced goods
- For some goods, difficulties in providing spare parts/repair services

Apart from trading (exporting), methods of entering foreign markets include the following.

- *Foreign direct investment (FDI):* this might involve buying or setting up a production facility in another country
- *Joint ventures* with overseas partners: these fall into two categories
    - *Industrial cooperation (contractual),* which is for a fixed period in which the parties' duties and responsibilities

are defined in a contract - common in the automotive industry, where economies of scale are large

  - *Joint equity*, which is of no fixed duration - may be the only feasible entry strategy into countries where full foreign ownership is discouraged

- *Licensing* involves conferring rights to make use of a production process in the overseas market in return for royalty payments: this can present problems of quality control, technology transfer leakages to competitors and the possibility of the licensee competing with the licensor in some markets

- *Management contracts*, whereby a firm agrees to sell management skills, are sometimes used in combination with licensing

Economic interest groups are organisations set up to help parties to joint ventures cooperate with one another and to overcome the problems which can arise from differences in local legislation and culture.

Risks 5/97

The special risks of international operations can be categorised as follows.

- *Foreign exchange risk,* whose management we have already considered

- *Geographical separation risk,* which adds to the problems of management control

- *Political risks and country risks,* including the following
  - Introduction of import quotas and tariffs, or non-tariff barriers, such as restrictive quality standards

- Nationalisation of foreign-owned assets by the host government, with or without compensation
- New regulations to restrict foreign shareholdings
- New exchange control regulations, eg limiting remittance of funds

Most assessments of political risk are at the macroeconomic country level. It is, however, important to assess the particular risks of individual projects.

Multinationals

A *multinational enterprise* is one which owns or controls production facilities or service facilities outside the country in which it is based. Larger examples include Ford, General Motors and Exxon (all US-based).

For what strategic reasons do companies engage in multinational investment (or 'FDI')? Companies may do so because they are seeking:

- Markets
- Raw materials
- Production efficiency
- Knowledge
- Political safety

Strategic reasons for FDI seem to weigh more heavily than financial considerations.

The Hymer-Kindleberger theory of FDI sees imperfections in product markets and factor markets as opening the way to FDI. Market imperfections might be created by:

- *Firms* (eg through product differentiation by creating brands)

- *Governments* (eg through tariff and non-tariff barriers, preferential procurement policies and exchange controls)

There have been changes in the pattern of FDI over recent years.

- The destination countries have changed, with a shift towards FDI in the 'NICs' (newly industrial countries) by companies based in the USA and elsewhere
- Reasons for FDI have changed. Production efficiency seeking has become more important, market seeking and raw material seeking less important
- Control of multinationals' production activities has become more centralised
- International integration ('globalisation') of capital markets has encouraged FDI

Transfer prices

Eventually any profit from an overseas venture must be remitted to the home country so that these can be passed to shareholders.

There are the following ways of doing this other than the obvious one of the subsidiary paying dividends to the parent.

- Loan interest
- Royalties
- Management charges
- Transfer pricing arrangements

Where it provides a means of remitting profits to the home country, *transfer pricing* is clearly of great importance to multinational enterprises.

The attractions of setting up a subsidiary in a tax haven, as opposed to a branch of the UK company, may be limited because of the UK tax rules on controlled foreign companies (CFCs).

Tax rules also govern sales at artificial transfer prices.

- Where sales are made to a non-resident fellow group company at an undervalue, or purchases are made from such a company at an overvalue, the Inland Revenue will substitute a market price in computing the profits chargeable to corporation tax
- However, no corresponding relief is given for sales at overvalue or purchases at undervalue by the UK company

The problem of transfer pricing has *motivational aspects* too.

To avoid motivational problems in a system of profit centre accounting, transfer prices need to be set at levels which will encourage profit centre managers to make decisions about inter-divisional transfer of goods and services that are in the best interests of the organisation as a whole.

Performance measurement

Performance measurement in an international group presents special problems.

- Foreign exchange translation needs to be made using a particular method
- Very different economic environments may be faced by different subsidiaries
- Caution is needed in making comparisons in a highly diversified group, as many multinationals are

Budget analysis - the comparison of sales and operating expenses with an earlier budget making use of price and volume variances - is probably the best way of measuring performance of subsidiaries in multinationals. Operating management is held *responsible* only for the variables influencing performance which they can control.

International portfolio diversification

International portfolio diversification provides a way of reducing the level of unsystematic risk compared with a purely domestic portfolio.

Can the investor achieve international portfolio diversification by investing in the shares of a multinational company?

Unlike a portfolio of stocks drawn from different international markets, the share price behaviour of multinational companies generally closely reflects that of non-multinational domestic firms.

The reduction of risk (ie the reduction in the variance of portfolio return) which international portfolio diversification can achieve is therefore not likely to be gained through the strategy of investing in a home-based multinational.

> *Exam focus.* Parts of a question on appraisal of an international investment could ask you to discuss some of the issues covered in this chapter.

International investment appraisal 5/95, 11/98

Appraising an overseas project involves similar principles to domestic investment appraisal, with some additional special considerations.

- Two sets of cash flows may need to be considered
    - Those earned by the overseas project
    - Those remitted to the parent company - these are generally the more important, since they accrue to the holding company shareholders
- Treatment will depend upon the discount rate used
    - Return required for the project in the foreign country - the present value could then be converted at the spot rate at time 0
    - Return required for foreign investment by parent company investors - this requires a projection of future exchange rates to convert into the domestic currency
- Adjustment of the discount rate may be required if the project has a different systematic risk compared with the company's existing activities, which may require the use of CAPM
- Restrictions on remittances - if these are likely, it can help to use local currency loans
- Changing exchange rates - you may need to predict changes in exchange rates based on purchasing power parity theory (see Chapter 28-29 above)
- Different inflation rates in the different countries
- Different tax systems
- Political risk (see earlier in this chapter)

Exporting to foreign countries may provide a means of growth when the domestic market for a company's products is saturated.

Foreign trade - importing from and exporting to foreign countries - involves the following risks.

- Physical risk
- Credit risk
- Exchange rate risk
- Trade risk (the overseas customer may refuse ownership or payment)
- Political risk

Payment and finance

Methods of settlement and finance for foreign trade include the following.

Bills of exchange. The exporter can get cash quickly by discounting the bill. If a bill is dishonoured, the drawer can take legal action in the drawee's country. The buyer's bank may guarantee payment of a term bill at maturity *('avalising')*.

Documentary letters of credit. Although slow to arrange, this method of payment is virtually risk-free, provided the exporter follows all the terms and conditions. The letter of credit is issued by the buyer's bank.

Forfaiting. This normally provides medium-term finance for exporters of capital goods. The exporter receives a down payment followed by a series of drafts or promissory notes which can be discounted by the exporter's bank (forfaiting bank).

Export factoring (or *international factoring*). This is similar to the factoring of domestic trade debts and is widely regarded as an appropriate means of trade finance and collection of receivables for small and medium-sized exporters.

Export credit insurance provides protection against the risk of non-payment by foreign customers.

> *Exam focus.* You could be asked to discuss which foreign trade finance methods are most appropriate for a particular company.

Countertrade

Countertrade is a general term used to describe various forms of 'barter' trading between companies or other organisations (eg state controlled organisation) in two or more countries. Note the following points.

- The volume of countertrade has grown to form around 10% - 15% of total international trade
- For organisations in heavily indebted countries which are short of foreign currency and credit facilities, it is sometimes the only way of arranging international trade
- Countertrade deals are typically complex, rarely involving simply a two-party barter arrangement

Notes